TACTICAL PAUSE

90 Days of
Combat Veteran Mentorship
to Guide Your Journey to Success

A.J. POWELL
US Army, Ret.

Heroes Media Group

www.heroesmediagroup.com

CONTENTS

FOREWORD

Tactical Pause: /ˈtaktɪk(ə)l pɔːz/ adverb. – *Taking a brief period to stop and engage in critical evaluation or consideration over actions carefully planned to gain a specific end, with intent to gauge effectiveness, potential, or alternative courses of action, before continuing on with the current operation(s), using those critical evaluations or considerations to adjust as necessary in order to accomplish the mission.*

Leaders routinely take a tactical pause before moving on to the next phase of operations, any time there's a shift in dynamics, and even purposely to criticize their own ideas, concepts, and decisions, to check for possible flaws, before actually putting them into action. A tactical pause is your opportunity to briefly critically evaluate a process, a plan, an idea, to second-guess yourself, or even – as this book is intended for use – as a tool to evaluate your own personal growth. And that's exactly what this concept is, a "tool" for you to use in your own endeavor toward self-betterment.

To that end, this book is meant to be used for daily inspiration of the reader toward his or her own personal and professional growth, essential to the core of the process of leadership development. The contents of this book are the result of decades of personal growth, professional development, adversity, trials and hardships, lessons learned, perseverance, dedication, sacrifice, and LDRSHIP. This book is the original work of the author, and source citations have been made throughout as appropriate to give credit to original sources, however, it is not the intent here to claim complete originality with any single thought process or development that could not readily be tied to an original source. Rather, it is the purpose of this book to do what Leaders do best... Provide Purpose,

Direction, and Motivation, and to Teach, Coach, Mentor, and Guide.

Each day's reading is a short thought or idea, lesson or concept, meant to guide the readers' own personal growth. In and of themselves, each reading lacks the depth required for a true and complete analysis, and makes no effort toward lengthy discussion and conceptualization of each subject or concept either. This book wasn't meant for that. Instead, the purpose is to provide the reader simple daily guided thoughts, to enable the reader to begin their own analysis, to inspire the reader to take their own actions, to motivate the reader to want to learn more, and to encourage the reader to be willing to apply them to their own lives.

Therefore, readers are tasked to perform their own considerations, personal reflection, application, and critical self-evaluation of each reading as they progress through the book. It is advised to take a few minutes at the beginning of each day, read only one chapter, then allow yourself to consider the message, reflect on how it can apply to your own life, apply its principles as able, and then briefly evaluate your personal effectiveness and growth. Continue reading a new chapter each day, repeating this process, and evaluating your personal growth over time. The hope is that you'll be realistic, and see honest results.

INTRODUCTION

Oh, I fully get that I'm a nobody. Merely one voice in billions. Compared to those people out there who are popular amongst the masses, I'm an unheard voice and an unknown face. But guess what? I don't do what I do to seek out "popularity". If I did, I'd be just as corrupt, shallow, and hypocritical as the vast majority of those who seek attention. I don't need to swear, gossip, or follow popular trends and fads just to reach my goal, nor do I need to bow down to mediocrity either. No, what I strive for can't be reached without honest hard work and sacrifice.

So, let's set get something straight right from the beginning here... I work daily to better myself; I seek out opportunities for exceptionalism daily, and by consequence, hopefully my own actions and growth will motivate and inspire others to follow suit. The road behind me fuels the motivation I need to keep going. And despite seeing the road ahead, the end is nowhere in sight... Just as it should be.

The simple fact is, you don't need to be famous to be a leader, you don't need millions of followers to inspire others either. You don't need to be a CEO, a Commissioned Officer, a Supervisor, Program Manager, Director, Squad Leader, or have any title of any kind. What you need is a personal desire to learn daily, the internal motivation to get started, a desire to succeed, the humility to accept growth, and the intestinal fortitude to press on, even when times are the toughest. When it comes to running the race, your starting line SHOULD be everyone else's finish line, and that's what sets the exceptional apart from the mediocre.

Throughout my career, I was blessed with opportunities to attend some of the hardest schools and courses the military has to offer, to be part of some amazing teams, filled with truly exceptional individuals, capable of accomplishing great and meaningful things. We didn't make it to where we were because we were all the hardest, strongest, fastest, smartest guys there were. We earned our right to come together because we were driven internally with an immeasurable desire to succeed, to continuously learn, to overcome adversities, to seek growth opportunities, and despite all odds, find a way to succeed. When the road looked the toughest, when the lights grew dim, when the day had given us its worst, and even after we gave it everything we had, we had an iron will to keep on going, and an internal drive to overcome any adversity to reach the goal.

Individuals of great character are molded by adversity, and it's the trials, not the sunshine, that grow us the most. Leaders aren't "leaders" because of those that follow them. It's the humility to admit there's always room for growth, the willingness to start the journey knowing full-well there is no end, the morale-boosting positive attitude that finds silver linings, the tenacity to try again (and again, and again), the braving of harsh elements to bring another back home, and even placing of the needs of the team ahead of their own to achieve goals. That's just a tiny fraction of what makes leaders "leaders", and through it all, individuals of great character are born, renowned and revered, and hailed as those WORTH following.

So, if you want to be a leader, if you want to reach your goals, if you want to achieve success in your life, you need to *BE* the example, *KNOW* your job, mission, and your purpose, and *DO* what's right. Put one foot in front of the other, take complete responsibility over your own life, hold yourself fully accountable for your actions, put in the hard work, and earn your way each and every day. Set your Bar of Standards forever just barely out of reach, and let it force you to forever strive for greater heights trying to reach it. By doing so, you'll lead by example, and the world will follow. So, be sure to set the right example, and the bar as high as you can.

Our journey will be a mixture of good and bad, of bliss and horror, of happiness and sadness... Accept it. Accept that life doesn't really care about you, but that doesn't mean you shouldn't care about yourself, those around you, your family, the team, or achieving the success you dream of. The reality is, that the world is a cold, harsh, desperate place, and life is filled with oceans to cross, mountains to climb, and storms to face. Yet no matter what life throws at us, no matter what adversity may cross our paths, no matter how many times, no matter how hopeless it may seem... Quitting is the only assurance that you'll never reach the goal, never accomplish the mission, never survive. So, when times are the toughest, it is you, and only you, who is the deciding factor on whether or not you'll rise to the challenge or suffer defeat.

What matters most in life is not whether or not we survive the hardships and trials that cross our path, it's how we choose to face them when we encounter them. And we will encounter them. Do we claim victimhood and fall prey to defeat, suggesting that the world is responsible for all our woes? Or do we smile regardless, grow a spine, develop some intestinal fortitude, take responsibility and accountability, grit through it, and find opportunities for growth in spite of it all? Do we wallow in self-pity? Or do we derive strength through our adversities, and use it as a tool to reach success, achieve greatness, and become better than we were the day before?

Simply don't quit! Because it's the point at which you think you have given it all you got and have nothing left to give that you'll find the starting line. That is where you'll discover what you're truly made of. That is when the real journey finally begins.

I may have never been the strongest or the fastest... But my starting line is most people's finish line... So here is my personal challenge to you...

If you think you can keep up, I dare you to try.

—A.J. POWELL
SSG, USA (Ret.)
Flyer, Diver, Combat Force Multiplier

90-DAY READINGS

FOUNDATION BUILDING DAYS

SO, YOU DECIDED TO BE SOMEBODY TODAY...

So, you FINALLY made the choice to commit yourself to BEING something MORE than what you are TODAY...

That's GREAT! But how are YOU going to get there?

How are you going to reach your goals? What are you going to do when the road gets tough? When the path gets hard? When the goal looks out of reach and the lights get dim?

Let me tell you something... Life doesn't CARE about you and being SUCCESSFUL at life is HARD!

Life is like a series of storms... One second you could be basking in the sun, the next slammed by the waves! Life doesn't care if you're weak, it doesn't care if you've had no sleep, and it couldn't care less if you're tired and ready to quit! One after the next, the storms WILL come! And what matters MOST in life is NOT whether you've survived the storms, it's how you faced them when they came!

Understand this: Adversity is quite possibly life's greatest teacher! If you would only listen, you would hear the wisest words in existence. That EVERY hardship is a lesson, every setback an opportunity for growth... That the ONLY thing that will EVER keep YOU from success is YOU!

When the chips are down, do you cry in self-pity? Or do you stand up, stare life right in the face, and give it all you got? Because it is THAT attitude that creates achievement! It's THAT attitude that creates success! It's THAT attitude that unlocks your potential!

Success is about BEING the example! Your potential is limited ONLY by your willingness to seek out challenges and strive for improvement. THERE ARE NO SECRETS! THERE ARE NO TRICKS! IT'S HARD WORK! PLAIN AND SIMPLE AS THAT! You have to be ready, willing, and able to hit the ground running and EARN YOUR TITLE EVERY SINGLE DAY! You have to leave your comfort behind you and learn to become comfortable with BEING uncomfortable!

You have to embrace the pain! Embrace the struggle! And be willing to go the distance! To lead from the front! Because the goal is a LOT easier to see from the FRONT of the pack than it is from the back! So, if you can step off the starting line on the path to your dreams, you need to KNOW you can make it across the finish line too!

It doesn't matter if it's a mile or a hundred miles! With the right attitude, you've already won! All YOU need to do is show up! HEY! 90% of LIFE is just SHOWING UP! If you'd simply just show up, the rest is easy!

Most people believe success is impossible! But I'm here to tell YOU that there is no such thing as "impossible"! When confronted with life's seeming impossibilities, I want to hear you say, "I GOT THIS!" and prove to the WORLD that the impossible is very possible indeed!

Now believe me when I say again, that it's not going to be easy... After all, NOTHING worth ANYTHING MEANINGFUL in life EVER comes easy! But we wouldn't want it any other way, now would we? NO! A reward for which we didn't work hard for has no luster, does it? The path to greatness, the road to achievement, the journey to success is harder than any other you'll ever encounter.

It is only when you've given it everything you got, when you're drained and exhausted and have nothing left to give, THAT is when you finally find out what you're truly made of! THAT is when you finally start to grow! THAT is when the REAL journey finally begins!

The road to success in life is long, it is difficult, it is painful, it is often lonesome and without end in sight, but there has NEVER been a statue erected for either critic OR coward! REMEMBRANCE IS THE REWARD FOR GREATNESS! Not for the lazy, weak willed, or frail of mind!

So BE brave!

Stare life right in the face and shout, "You can't keep me down! I will march on! I will NEVER quit! I will NEVER surrender! I will never stop moving forward! I will pick up my weapon and fight! And I WILL give it all I got!" Because THAT's how you win! THAT's how you achieve! THAT's how you become successful at life!

That's what it takes to achieve greatness.

After all, it's the content of your character that will ultimately become the key to your success or the linchpin of your demise.

NO ONE is capable of walking your journey except YOU! So NEVER be afraid to take that next step...

And *THAT* is what this book – and your daily, self-motivated development – is all about.

FIND YOUR PURPOSE

The definition of "Leadership" is: The process of influencing people by providing Purpose, Direction, and Motivation, while operating to accomplish the mission, and improve the organization. (US Army, ADP 6-22)

There is so very much in that one sentence that entire books have been written on expanding and detailing every facet of possible study from within its words. Of course, the truth behind the nature of this definition is found it its reverse order.

To accomplish the mission and improve the organization, people need to be motivated to want to achieve and grow. Before real motivation can sprout, people need a direction for which to apply their efforts. They need a vision, an objective, a common goal to reach and strive for.

Yet even that is not enough. Before a team will even take to striving for the goal, it must be made meaningful to them. Why in the world should they care? Why should they work so hard to get there? Why must they endure hardships and trials, move mountains and cross oceans to reach it? What makes people willing to embark on a journey to achieve great and meaningful things, and strive for exceptionalism?

It's Purpose.

When it comes to getting a team to achieve success, they need to have a purpose. Combine that purpose with the provision of direction and careful guidance and mentorship, and you can cultivate real motivation. And a highly motivated team can accomplish anything.

Let me tell you... So often we hear managers try to remind us of our "duty" when attempting to create false motivation within us so the team can at least reach the goal. Well, my friends, this is why they are "managers", and not "leaders". For "Duty" alone is a very poor motivator.

When you've trekked for miles on end, haven't eaten in a very long time, are dirty and sweaty, tired and sore, a sense of "duty" is the last thing you'll turn to just to help get you through. You have a mission to accomplish, a job to do, and others are depending on you. There must be something far deeper and more meaningful than "duty" that's driving you and motivating you to keep going.

You need a purpose.

A sense of meaningful purpose is what drives people of all kinds to reach unfathomable heights, to come together and accomplish great and meaningful things. Purpose motivates people to brave a hail of lead to save a life, to jump into the open ocean to pull a survivor to safety, to take the risk, tread new paths, blaze new trails, and to set the standard higher than ever before.

Without a purpose to move us, we waste away. Loss of motivation will occur with forgetfulness of purpose, and without that motivation to push us along, we quit. Quit on our projects, our self-progression, our jobs, the mission, others, ourselves, and sometimes, even life itself.

So, ask yourself, in all seriousness... Do you want to climb that mountain before your eyes?! Are you ready for the next evolution?! Do you want to make a difference, create a real impact, and change lives?

THEN FIND YOUR PURPOSE!

Grab hold of it with all you got, and when your body gives out, you press on! Because your mind is strong, and KNOWING your purpose, you can still go on.

Today, consider carefully your purpose, whatever it may be. Just spend five or ten minutes by yourself in solemn personal reflection, be one hundred percent completely honest with yourself, and explore your purpose.

You may discover that you might not have one yet. If that sounds like you, if after taking a cold, hard, honest look at yourself you discover you really haven't found a purpose yet, you've probably been going through life up to this point aimlessly, like a tumbleweed in the wind, carried along by the whims of chance and circumstance. To this I say, what a sad waste of potential.

But fear not! For with this realization, now's the perfect time to flesh out what you want most out of your life! And so long as that vision amounts to something positive, that improves the world around you and inspires others to achieve, then let THAT become your purpose!

You may also discover that you have found a purpose, but you have yet to clearly define what exactly it is. That's ok too! At least you've already identified something meaningful enough to you that you're willing to dedicate your efforts toward! Explore it, write it down, brainstorm upon it, and develop it until you have finally fully conceptualized it clearly.

What is your purpose? Why is it important to you? Why might it be important to others? Can it solve a pressing problem or issue? Will it improve your life or the lives of others? Is it truly worth spending a lifetime working toward? Your purpose need not be set in stone. It can be adaptable, and I promise you, as you grow older, it will slowly evolve. But that's a conversation for another time...

For now, simply spend today reflecting on these questions, and work on clearly defining your purpose. It will make all the difference in the days to come.

CORE VALUES

- Loyalty, Duty, Respect, Selfless-service, Honor, Integrity, and Personal Courage (LDRSHIP) (U.S. Army Core Values).
- Honor, Courage, and Commitment (U.S. Navy and Marine Corps Core Values).
- Integrity, Service, and Excellence (U.S. Air Force Core Values)

Whatever they may be, clearly identifying and defining your core values is possibly the most essential aspect of beginning your development as a growing leader and an individual striving to attain a measure of success in life. Before we can decide on a direction to take in life, we need to clearly articulate what exactly it is we believe in and what we will stand for no matter the cost. What are our individual, fundamental beliefs? Core values are the guiding principles that dictate our behavior, our decisions, our thought processes, and our inherent biases. They are what we derive our own morals from, helping us to distinguish between right and wrong, and from there, aid in our understanding of both personal and professional ethics.

Very often, however, most people in the beginning stages of their journey to success struggle with trying to clearly conceptualize their own core values, and then articulate them in a well-defined way. As a result, we often tend to look outside of ourselves to find external sources from which to borrow core values from until we can begin to define our own. For example, my own personal core values are a mixture of Christian values taught in God's Word, those instilled on me from my parents, and those gained from a lifetime growing up in, and subsequently serving, in the United States Navy and Army.

Just understand that borrowing values is natural in the beginning, and you'll find that as you age, your own personal core values will begin to surface and take shape. You may choose to hold on to those you've borrowed, modify them to your own image, or let them go completely in favor of something else. Whatever the case may be, understand that, like most of the concepts in this book, these things will take time and considerable effort on your part. If you started your journey thinking this would be easy or that you'll finish quickly, you've entered into your journey with a fundamentally flawed mentality. If that's you, I've got a rude awakening for you... This will take a lifetime, and there is no "end". Your goal rests at the top of a Mountain with No Summit, but we'll get to that in time.

For today, focus on trying to conceptualize your own personal core values. What will you stand for no matter what? What do you believe in without question or doubt? Write your ideas down. Try to reduce each value into a single word or short sentence and go from there. It's ok if they're not your own or not original to you. But remember this: Your core values are a direct reflection of who you are as a person and as a leader, and they will come out in your personality, decisions, and actions. So, think hard, and think carefully. Who are YOU, and what do YOU believe in? THAT is the question to consider today.

LOYALTY

Often a term cast into a conversation without much thought, as if it were pocket change used to make up the remainder not covered by a larger sum, "Loyalty" has been reduced to mere conversational or anecdotal filler in our age. Our use of loyalty in professional reference has become fodder to fill space, as addendum to referencing of character, or as detraction in the chronology of an individual's history. Yet loyalty used to mean so much more, and the mention of it once carried strong emotional attachment and connotation alike. To be "loyal" to someone or something, to a cause or purpose, a friend or an organization, used to carry real weight, and those found lacking this quality discovered themselves as outcasts and untrustworthy persons.

What society seems to have long forgotten is the true meaning behind the word; loyalty to country, unit, family, and self; to core values and to the mission. Being loyal means you'll be there when needed most, to answer the call when called upon, that you can be trusted with matters of great importance and to complete the task – even when no one is watching – that you'll support your teammates through thick and thin, or be there to aid a person you've never met. Loyalty is a serious act of commitment, and the mere mention of it used to indicate a person worthy of respect and praise. Alas, fewer and fewer individuals these days truly understand and covet this word, and often it's those who have lived its meaning on a daily basis for a prolonged period of time. Those who would have sacrificed everything for it, given their all to protect it, and have devoted themselves honorably to it.

Might you be among them?

Today, take some time to ponder, to as great an extent as you can fathom, the depth and essence of the word "loyalty". What does it mean to you? How does it apply to your life today? How should it apply tomorrow? What is it you're loyal to? Your nation? An organization? A unit or team? Are you loyal to your family? Your friends? To your principles, values or your faith? Ask yourself this… If it meant the difference between sacrificing everything – up to and including your very life – would you do it to stay "loyal" to those things? Consider carefully your immediate answer.

Those same individuals mentioned above, those who understand and covet this word because they've lived it, are some of the same who have done exactly that. Imagine, if you can, the magnitude and depth of value they placed in this word, to sacrifice life for it so that the team would survive, so that a child might live, so that the mission would be successful, so that your life might be saved… There are people out there right now, dedicated to their loyalty to you through extension of their service, and they don't even know you personally…

What does loyalty mean to you? THAT is the question to consider today.

DUTY

Life is filled with obligations, routine requirements, tasks that simply must be performed, and even moral and legal responsibilities that take up our time. Throughout the typical year, obligations consume a significant portion of our days. Yet while there are many requirements we can live without – and surely there exist plenty of opportunity for simplification, automation, and streamlining – many are entirely necessary for the world to function, and for your life to function. However, make no mistake about it, we do have a choice... Despite the fact that life's obligations take up our precious time, we have choices in how we decide to view them, as well as in how we utilize them.

For the most part, people generally tend to think of duties as obligations they can live without. They see them negatively as menial tasks that are a waste of their time and a drain of their efforts. But what many fail to understand is that reaching our goals most often requires the efforts of a team, and dedicated effort from each member is essential for the team to succeed. Duty, therefore, is made up of the complex combination of missions, tasks, and individual responsibilities – all constantly in motion – that we carry out faithfully to assure team success. And when the team succeeds, we succeed.

Additionally, while obligations tend to appear routine and fruitless, a myriad of opportunities exist in the shadows for fruitful productivity. Indeed, the concept of "Duty" extends well-beyond merely chores and routine tasks, and into the very fabric of our own personal development. We have both external and internal obligations, and just as you may have a duty to your teams' success, you also have a duty to your own success as well. This means you have an obligated commitment to achieve new goals and reach new heights, to continuous, daily self-improvement, to take care of your health and well-being, to grow your mind, body, and soul... A duty to lead by example.

"Duty", therefore, is no longer a negative restraint eating away at your life, now is it? No... "Duty" is the dedicated effort we use to faithfully meet our obligation to grow.

Today, take some time to consider how you choose to view the obligations of your life. Are they beasts of burden? Bringers of pessimism? Roadblocks preventing you from doing what YOU want to do? Or are they commitments to the mission? Opportunities to remain dedicated? The cogs that keep us pushing forward toward achievement and reaching the goal? Of course, not ALL "duties" are necessary in life, and indeed a great majority can be disposed of or automated, leaving you free-er to dedicate your time toward more meaningful ventures... But for those responsibilities that remain, those you just can't live without... Are they unfortunate matters of existence? Or are they drivers that keep you moving forward?

RESPECT

Respect is earned, yet it can also be given. It's a two-way street, but it's also a sign of good character. You can have respect for a person or merely the position. Respect comes in many forms, but none can ever be attained by demand. It's our hard work that gains it, the bonds we make that nurture and grow it, and our dedication that maintains and sustains it. It's the trust we've placed in others, and the vital ingredient making up the valuation of your own self-worth. It's one of the building blocks for mutuality of concern within your team, and the knowledge that you've put forth your best effort each day.

It goes without saying that "Respect" is a vital ingredient to success, and not just for your own success, but for that of an entire team as well. When others freely give it to you, it's a sign you're doing a good job. When you have it for yourself, it's a sign you believe you're doing your best. And when you give it to others, it's a sign of trust that they are capable, valued, and worthy of your time.

Yet for all these things, it's highly important to point out the sheer magnitude of abuse the word "respect" has suffered in our age. Far too many use it to demand special treatment from those they view as below them in status either personally and/or professionally. Far too many use it to make pathetic claims of victimhood when someone else didn't live up to their previously unannounced yet impossibly high level of self-entitlement. Far too many withhold giving it to someone when they believe that person should have shown it toward them first – effectively weaponizing the word. And far too many use it as a tool to subdue and oppress others through extension of a position, title, or office.

"Respect" should be something positive, a confirmation of value, trust, loyalty, commitment, and a proven track record, amongst other things, and it was once a social norm, a sign of proper upbringing and personal maturity... A person who readily shows respect for others is an individual of good character, and as such, respectable themselves. Yet in the wrong hands, the word can become a twisted, malicious tool used to suppress, oppress, and attack others. It has largely ceased being a part of our default social custom, and instead, has been replaced with self-entitlement.

Today, take some time to carefully consider how the word "respect" applies to your life. It should NEVER be seen from the perspective of "how" or "why" other people should respect you... No... Your consideration should AT ALL TIMES focus on a perspective of how YOU respect others. Do you show proper respect for those around you? For those in a position of authority? For those who earned it? Do you respect the property of others? Do you respect life? Individual Faiths? The rule of law? Your friends, family, and most importantly of all... Do you respect yourself?

How does "respect" apply to you? I guarantee you'll discover, the more freely you give it, the better your life – and the lives of those around you – will become.

SELFLESS SERVICE

John 15:13 (KJV) – "Greater love hath no man than this, that a man lay down his life for his friends."

Many have heard life's Call to Service, few have answered that call, and fewer still have paid the ultimate price living up to that call. Whether it be to family and friends or a stranger in need, to an organization or a team, to a community or the entire nation, mission success is made possible only by the selfless dedication of those willing to serve. The willingness to place the needs of others before yourself is the sacrificial mindset that spawns courageous action, timeless endurance, and heroic measures of humanity... It's the silent driver to achieving success, and we often fail to realize the selflessness of those who serve us with their time and efforts.

When most initially think of "selfless service", they often look immediately toward society's most obvious examples – the firefighter who runs into a burning building to save a child, the medic who works tirelessly to stop bleeding, the officer who patrols the most violent streets to make them safer, and the service member who takes the fight to the enemy to protect the nation... Yet selfless service is seen every day in the mechanic who double-checks their work to assure the aircraft is safe to fly, the doctor who stays up late to study charts that may save a life, the teacher who gives extra attention to a struggling student, and even the parent who stays up late to help that student with their homework. From the custodian who faithfully maintains the building, to the city worker who struggles during a raging storm to restore utilities, every person is a valued member of a greater whole, and it takes their commitment to serve something bigger than themselves for society to function, grow, and prosper.

As such, selfless service doesn't always equal putting yourself in harm's way or making the ultimate sacrifice… Indeed, the term "laying down his life" can be extended to a spectrum of dedicated actions taken to benefit another positively without any personal gain for the self. It's a dedication carried out in daily duties and the extra effort put into the little things that typically add up to the most common examples of service to the greater whole. When there remains no real benefit to the individual, when the effort required for another to succeed comes at a cost to yourself, therein rests the opportunity for service, and we find the truest definition simply stated as: Putting the welfare of the nation, the organization, the team or another individual before your own.

Today, take some time to reflect on your own "service"… What do you willingly serve? Who do you serve? Do you place the needs of your family before your own? Do you let them eat first at mealtimes? Help with homework and chores? Do you stay late to assure the project at work is completed on time? Do you double-check your work just to be sure it was done right the first time? Do you serve your community through volunteering or as a profession? Do you place the needs of another, the team, the organization, and the mission before your own? Ask yourself, "How do you serve", and if you can't find an example of service in your life, perhaps it's time to consider opportunities to start.

HONOR

The total encompassment of all other values, "Honor" is a matter of carrying out, acting, and living the core values to which you are held to as the minimum standard of your daily life. Honor is not an act, it isn't a choice you decide to make, it's not a prize to be won, nor is it something you can give. It's an earned quality, a state of being, built over time and retained by steady commitment.

You can't have honor if you compromise your values. Individuals who choose to sacrifice their values for personal gain will quickly be found lacking this quality, and those found without honor are often shunned as an outcast, rejected as individuals not worthy of trust or respect, strangers not belonging to the team, and failures incapable of success. Society tends to treat those lacking honor as criminals, degenerates, and scoundrels, lowlifes who would sacrifice others to save of themselves, who couldn't be counted on when it matters the most.

"Honor", therefore, is a very big deal and should matter greatly to you.

Living up to the standards of your core values on a daily basis and exemplifying yourself as a standard-bearer is the mark of a true leader. Honorable individuals are living guidons. They are bright beacons that light the way, praised for steadfast dedication, and hailed as the examples others strive to become themselves. To be found honorable is to have a reputation of uncompromising moral character, worthy of trust and respect, and prized as valued members of the team.

So, for today, think carefully... Are you an individual who can be found honorable?

Forget the whole concept for a moment, and ask instead, do you faithfully live up to the core values you're held to on a daily basis? Do your actions stand as a testament of good moral character? Do you strive consistently to maintain higher standards for yourself based on those values, and without wavering, hold yourself fully accountable to keep them regardless of the situations in which you find yourself? Before answering these questions, ask yourself the reverse... Was there ever a time when you knew full well that you failed to live up to your standards and values? Consider carefully the circumstances... Nobody's perfect, and it's imperative to understand that. Even in failure, there is honor in learning from personal mistakes, yet no honor can be found in those who fail to live up to their values, then refuse to admit it and/or refuse to learn from their own personal shortcomings.

A dishonorable person is incapable of leadership and growth, achievement may never be within their grasp, and the measure of success in life they dream of for themselves may forever elude them because of it. So, consider carefully all of the values, obligations, and standards you have for yourself, as well as those placed upon your shoulders, and ask yourself seriously... Do you strive daily to live up to them? If you find yourself lacking, don't be dismayed, for a new opportunity has presented itself for you to be found with honor.

INTEGRITY

Contrary to popular misrepresentation, "Integrity" has nothing to do with "telling the truth" or "doing the right thing", and everything to do with consistency. It's common for people to suggest that a person who lied about something or willingly committed a wrongful act has "no integrity", yet this is a gross misuse of the word... "Integrity" simply means "to remain consistent with one's actions and values". An individual can have horrible personal values, and so long as they remain consistent with those values, they indeed do have integrity. Similarly, so long as they maintain consistency in their actions, and those actions agree or align with their values, here too do they keep and maintain their own personal integrity. Yet this is only one-half of the total equation...

Just like our previous discussion on "Honor" highlighted, we have our own personal values, as well as values placed upon us from outside of ourselves. We have professional values, organizational values, team values, family values, values based on core beliefs and Faith, and even values between friends. All of these different sources may have significant overlap between shared values that intersect with our own and each other, and some may have outliers that are unique to themselves, yet none of that changes the fact that we're obligated to uphold them so long as we maintain a commitment to the source that enacts them.

Further complicating the matter is the fact that some values are fluid and based on socially-situationally dependent constructs. Meaning that the values one team or organization has that you belong to may not necessarily be the same values as another team or organization to which you also belong to. If the values of one side disagree with the values of the other, a conflict now exists whereby your integrity may be compromised should those two different sides clash. You very well may be forced to pick one side over the other in order to maintain your own integrity.

It would seem maintaining our own integrity is much more of a complicated task than initially thought, now isn't it?

Today, take some time to consider very carefully the consistency you maintain with the values you personally hold, and the values placed upon you. You'll likely find that there exist a number of cases where your own personal values and those of organizations and groups you belong to are the same. You'll also likely find that there exist a number of cases where they conflict. In those cases, how do you justify maintaining your integrity – both to yourself and to others? There is one simple way to know if you're on the right track...

Do what's right, morally and legally, at all times.

It may not always be easy to discern if you've managed to maintain consistency with all values placed upon you at all times, but so long as your actions are morally and legally just, you'll find that you're well within the scope of retaining your integrity. And if ever challenged on that fact, you'll be found spotless.

PERSONAL COURAGE

No issue will ever get resolved, no mystery ever solved, no obstacle or barrier or trial ever overcome, and no dreams ever achieved, without the courage to face them, deal with them, stand up to them, and chase them down. The simple truth of the matter is, the mere act of you walking your path on the journey to success in life will create conflict of all kinds, and the fact is... Conflict avoidance will never allow you to solve your problems, never help you to overcome hardships, and never allow you to reach your goals. Without the courage to face life head on, you'll accomplish nothing, amount to nothing, and lead no one.

When we come across conflict – whether internal or external, interpersonal or within a group dynamic – the singular source emotion that prevents most people from dealing with that conflict is "fear". People fear judgment, disagreement, the creation of more conflict, losing a friend or colleague, being "labeled" or shunned, ridiculed or treated as an outcast, and more. There exist entire societies where "conflict avoidance" is a daily cultural norm engraved into the very fabric of their cultural DNA (Japanese culture is largely this way), and the fear of disagreement often prevents necessary and much-needed actions to solve and fix problems and issues – both personally as well as professionally. Internally, we struggle with making decisions over a conflict within ourselves to either speak up or take action when we know we can or should. Fear is the largest emotional barrier preventing personal growth, professional achievement, and individual success. And yet, what most fail to realize, is that "Courage" is not the absence of fear. Absolutely not. No... Courage is the ability and willingness to take action despite fear. Therefore, it's perfectly acceptable to be afraid, but never acceptable to allow fear to control you and prevent you from taking action.

Personal courage comes in many forms and can be exhibited in many ways. Of course, the physical actions of courage are easy to identify. Pulling a survivor from a car wreck or burning building, operating in combat to accomplish the mission, and taking down an armed suspect are all fine examples of courage in action… But personal courage is found in every person who tries again (and again) despite failing, who stands up to a bully, who befriends a lonely classmate or coworker, who pushes through rehab from injuries despite the pain, who admits they have a problem and actively seeks help, who confides in a friend or family member their struggle, who puts personal issues aside to solve professional problems, who admits their faults and accepts accountability and responsibility for their own life and actions, and who commits seriously to personal and professional growth. When people confront and face life's fears, regardless of the possible consequences, that's courageousness, and it's a key that unlocks your potential to accomplish great and meaningful things.

Today, consider carefully what challenges – physical, mental, or spiritual – have you faced in life that required personal courage? Be honest. Did you fail to take action when you knew you should have? Were you frozen by fear, unable or unwilling to act? Or did you rise to the occasion despite fear? Then consider this… How will your personal courage affect your ability to achieve today and tomorrow? If you find your past examples indicated a lack of courage, don't dismiss this or feel ashamed… Embrace it and use it to change. If you find you had no problem taking action despite what might happen, consider if your actions were positive or negative and what possible alternatives might have been better. You might be surprised at what you find.

— Day 11 —

ENOUGH WITH EXCUSES

Today's the day you admit it out loud. Today's the day you accept the truth. So far you've contemplated getting your base values established, and started building your character to align with those values, but to continue progressing on your journey, you must now begin tearing down the biggest barrier preventing you from ever making real, honest, change and progress... Yourself. YOU are the ONE THING that will consistently, time and again, prevent you from reaching success and achieving your goals... And one of the worst ways you do this to yourself is by making excuses.

That's right! You read that correctly...

Up until this point in your life, I guarantee you've made any number of excuses in the past – to yourself and others – for why something didn't go as planned, didn't go the way you wanted it to, didn't get accomplished, why your New Year's resolutions weren't kept, why you still haven't finished that project, finished school, completed those assignments, cleaned the house, gotten into shape or started eating healthier. The truth is, most people are often highly change-resistant. They develop lifestyle habits, work habits, and mental biases that prevent them from growth, and they will come up with every excuse imaginable to shift blame onto anyone and anything else in order to avoid taking any kind of personal accountability and responsibility for their very own failures in life.

After all, most people don't like the idea of "failure". They see the word as something negative instead of something positive (which we'll eventually get to), and as such, will avoid the label at all cost. So, they make excuses. It wasn't their fault for why they didn't get that promotion, why they didn't make the cut, why they didn't get the grades... It wasn't their fault they haven't reached their goals or realized their dreams... No... It's "society's" fault! It's "life's" fault! It's "that supervisor's" fault! It's "the wealthy people's" fault! It's "the government's" fault! Right?

And then what happens? They start self-victimizing, they start suggesting they're the victim of some conspiracy to keep them down in order to reconcile to themselves that they aren't at fault for their failures and to justify to themselves and the world their current lack of life luster, don't they? Suddenly "the man" has kept them down, "society" has oppressed them, and "the system" is rigged against them...

Next, instead of looking at the real problem, instead of taking full responsibility and accountability for their own lives and decisions, they look outwardly, and in their blame of the world, they demand they're "entitled" to their dreams and success! They begin to suggest that the world owes them something, and to get it, they must steal it from someone or something that has "somehow" prevented them from attaining it! Yet... For the vast majority, they don't get what they demand, and what happens then? Well, that's the final stage... They slip into a pit of pessimism and self-loathing, hatred and contempt for the world, and fall into the belief that they will never achieve anything as they begin to give up entirely on their dreams...

Well enough is enough already... The excuses have got to stop! This constant game of self-defeatist, pity-party garbage has gone on for far too long in your life, hasn't it?! Just stop it already! We've talked about this countless times by now, right?!

It's well beyond time you stopped staring at the floor as you walk around and started standing tall and looking straight ahead! Past time you stopped suggesting you're not the best and started owning your accomplishments! Stop saying you can't do something and start asking "how" you can reach the goal! Stop pointing fingers at the world and start pointing at yourself! It's well beyond time you stopped making excuses for your life and started accepting responsibility and holding yourself accountable! It's NO ONE'S fault you're not where you want to be but YOURS! Not society's, not the governments, not any sex or race, background or belief... It's YOUR job to make YOU successful, and every time you make another excuse for why you can't or why you haven't, it's YOU who's defeating yourself!

GROW A SPINE and DEMAND the best of yourself for once, and you'll FINALLY realize that it's been YOU all along that has been blocking your progress! Stop looking at the world and start looking at yourself... YOU are the only person who can make your dreams come true, and you kill your opportunities with every excuse you make for why you have yet to reach them.

Today, contemplate very hard on all the excuses you've made in your life so far. You're not doing this exercise with anyone else, so you shouldn't be worried about what others might think. No... This is you being completely honest with yourself. You're the one who judges yourself the most anyway, so you might as well start using it to help you grow, right? Think very hard about the kind of excuses you typically make, the progression of mental states those excuse evolved into, and how they've affected your life so far... Then admit it... Admit to yourself that your failures are your responsibility, and accept accountability for those events in your life... For your actions or lack thereof. And finally, accept that, just because you may have failed in the past, doesn't automatically mean you're a failure. When you stop making excuses and start accepting personal responsibility for yourself, it is then that you can finally begin to break through the barriers that were once preventing you from making progress, and what you'll discover, is that you're finally able to move forward toward reaching your goals and achieving the success you dream of.

CHANGE YOUR PERSPECTIVE

When you look back at your life, are you proud at what you see? Have you worked hard for something worthwhile and meaningful? Have you created an impact and made a difference? After all, that's what most people are looking to find when they reflect on their past to determine if they've achieved a measure of success thus far... Right?

We see them every day all around us, countless individuals who wallow in self-pity over a belief that they haven't yet achieved something meaningful in life. The world is filled with young people who claim they want to "make a difference" and "create an impact", yet their ideas on how to accomplish these things are based on cheap, shallow dreams of grandeur and fame. All they ever think about is themselves, and as a result, the world is consequentially filled with people who are angered and depressed, disenchanted and apathetic, because they have yet to gain those shallow and cheap lofty dreams. You see... The truth is, that "creating a REAL impact", "making a REAL difference", and achieving something truly "meaningful" in life has far more to do with people and hard work than it does tangible riches or notoriety amongst the masses.

When we look at all of humanity's great achievements, from medical advancements to exploring outer space, they all have a few things in common... It took the collective effort of people working hard, people gaining and sharing knowledge, people helping and supporting each other, and people coming together as a team to make those things possible. Even the greatest athlete would fail without the help of coaches and expert trainers, sports dieticians and equipment managers, and more, to support their efforts. The General is nothing without his

Soldiers, the factory nothing without its supply chain, a pilot nothing without mechanics, and a visionary nothing without all the people who can make their vision a reality.

People and the relationships they share are what moves mountains, saves lives, and explores the universe... And if you'd simply start focusing on those things, you'll quickly discover your dreams closer than you realize. You can't make it through life without the help of others, and you'll never be successful without the help of others either. Once you change your perspective on what pieces are truly important to achieve success, your goals will suddenly become far easier to reach than most believe possible.

Today, take some time to carefully consider the relationships around you. Your family and friends, the groups and teams you belong to, and even the organizations you're a part of. If you think you'll eventually amount to something all on your own, you're sadly mistaken... All of these people are an important piece of your future success. They know things you don't, can see things you can't, are capable of things you aren't, and the reverse is the same for them. Consider carefully how you can nurture the relationships you have and be a part of a strong, cohesive team willing to work hard toward great and meaningful things, and you'll find you've impacted the lives of others along the way, made a difference in the world, and accomplished something meaningful as a result.

BEAT YOURSELF

To beat the odds, you first have to beat yourself. YOU are your own worst enemy. Your mind, the saboteur you never saw coming...

Imagine you're in the race of your life and you have a distance to go. You have no idea how far, but you know it's farther than you've ever gone before. Yet before you've even taken the first step, you've questioned your ability to make it... Shortly into the journey, and doubt has crept up on your every thought. Before you know it, you're weak, gasping for breath, sore, and sputtering on fumes with a near-empty tank, void of any motivation left to be had...

You defeated yourself before your journey ever began...

The road to success is cut short for most people in exactly this manner. Why is that? It's because your mind is the deciding factor in your internalized motivation to succeed, and it will quit on you, destroying even the remotest possibility of your success, LONG before your body EVER will!

Think about it. Have you ever ran a HUNDRED miles? Consider the distance and imagine actually running it. Most would dismiss the idea immediately, but consider full-on running for a hundred miles... It's very possible. People do it all the time. Could you make it?

What about swimming? Have you ever swam the open ocean for hours on end? Leaving the safety of land, braving rolling waves, with no bottom to touch and no idea what might be lurking in the unknown depths... What if your boat was sinking, and the only means of survival was to swim for miles over the horizon to reach land? You're more than capable, you just have to want it. Would you make it?

What about bouncing back from crippling permanent injuries? There are stories of amazing individuals who accomplish what medical professionals say isn't possible on a daily basis...

Consider this... When properly motivated, nothing can stand in your way. If your mind is tough, and your will is strong, you can overcome ANYTHING. You are so much more capable than you realize, and so few KNOW this to be a fact. The truth is, your ability to make the unknown distance of your journey depends entirely upon whether or not you truly believe you can make it. Sure, pushing yourself to the limits and beyond will be hard. Of course, there will be pain and discomfort, and it could be down-right agonizing! But you're fully capable of pushing past all that and making it to the other side, so long as you refuse to allow your mind to ever for a second suggest to you that you can't.

Today, take some time to think about all the times in your life you might have defeated yourself, all the times your mind fed you a diet of self-doubt and you ended up not completing a seemingly difficult task because of it. Then, consider all the individuals who succeeded in those tasks... It's not as if they were stronger, smarter, faster, or better than you, but I'm positive they didn't doubt they could make it either. Never allow self-doubt to sabotage you. You may not see the end, but you can make it. You just have to want it bad enough. It is not your job to fail... It's your job to be unstoppable, be exceptional, to never quit, and be successful.

STOP LIVING IN THE PAST

They say those who forget the past are doomed to repeat it... And while that is absolutely true, and learning about, understanding, and applying lessons learned from history is highly important to future success, not remaining stuck on that history is just as important.

We've all seen examples of individuals stuck living in the past, haven't we? The person who has rested on their laurels, the person who peaked in high school and hasn't accomplished anything worth noting since, the person who tells the same old war stories time and time again, the person who can't move on from the "glory days", and the person who drowns themselves in sorrow and misery, bitterness and anger, because of a past event they refuse to move on from... Being stuck on the past is like remaining standing at the starting line of a race that started long ago, or driving a car forward while focusing intensely on the rearview mirror. It's either a refusal to move forward and make progress, or a dangerous act of not paying attention to where you're going, but either way the result is the same... You'll never achieve anything in life if you can't move on from the past and refuse to look toward the future.

So, stop talking about the "you" of yesterday, stop dwelling on "what might have been", and stop wallowing on past events. What you accomplished yesterday doesn't matter anymore, the past won't change, no one cares who you used to be, and just because you might have had a bad experience or a missed opportunity doesn't mean you can't reach your dreams and achieve success tomorrow... Unless you refuse to act today. I'm not saying to simply forget about your history. Not at all. Your past is just as important as your present. You should be proud of your accomplishments and achievements, your struggles have made you strong and resilient, and the experiences of your life have helped to mold you into who you are today... But what I am saying, is that your past shouldn't be the focus of your present. Instead, it should be the driver of your present. You should learn from it – all of it, both the good and the bad – and use it as a tool to make yourself better. Our focus should be on the horizon looking toward the future, using the past as the building block that helps us move forward toward that future.

Today, take some time to consider your own past life experiences – both the good and the bad – and consider if you have been stuck living in the past, unable or unwilling to move forward at one time or another. Of course, we all cherish the good experiences of our life, but the real shapers of our character are the bad experiences – the ones filled with adversity and hardship. The majority of people try to forget them or dwell on them or let them taint their character... But successful people use bad past experiences to grow and achieve their future goals. They see them as learning opportunities, and as a result, those same bad experiences shape their character in a powerfully positive way, allowing those individuals to move on toward reaching their dreams. Don't let your life become a stagnant pond, never flowing or progressing. Don't let your past keep you from moving forward toward the greatness you're capable of. Instead, stay focused on the future, and use the past to help you get there.

THE CALL TO SERVICE

Like a firearm, an aircraft, a tank, an arrow, a knife, or any other instrument of warfare... A sword is just a tool used in the service of a cause bigger than itself. Though without the sword the battle could not be won, by itself the sword is useless. Swords are an extension of the warriors that wield them, and often inscribed upon the steel thereof, do we find a visual reminder of the truth... A name engraved... And that engraved mark proves the REAL "weapon" is the warrior the sword serves.

A true warrior goes forth into battle, not because we hate what stands before us... But because we love that which we protect behind us. And if you are ever to be victorious, like your tools, you must sharpen and maintain, hone and tone, polish and refine yourself... To be ever at the ready, and in the best condition possible, or you'll rust and waste away, and fail to serve when needed most. You must commit yourself to continuous improvement so that when the time comes to be that protector, you'll be a confident, competent, and capable member of the team. And to be successful in this endeavor, like the very sword you wield, you too must commit yourself to a life of service, to serving something bigger than yourself.

A call to service is a call of selflessness to a purpose... To the protection and defense of your family, friends, neighbors, and your very way of life. It's a call to placing the lives of others before your own, to serve Faithfully and Honorably, So Others May Live. It's a commitment to the team, to placing of the needs of the team before your own. To the organization, its mission, its improvement and growth, and its success. And to your relationships, to the service of your family and friends... To truly serve something is to truly love something. "Greater love hath no man than this, that a man lay down his life for his friends..." We see the relationship of service and personal sacrifice tied directly to love throughout all of human history and given this tied relationship we can say for certain, just as no man wishes for peace more than the Soldier, no man loveth more than he who willingly serves.

Just like the path of the warrior is a commitment to a life of service, so too is the path of leadership a commitment to service as well – service to the mission and the cause, to the team and to the journey... The journey to success.

Today, consider carefully whom you serve... Do you serve the team, the organization, or the nation? Do you serve your family and friends, carefully tending to the growth of those bonds as a gardener tends to their garden? Do you serve God?

Or do you only serve yourself...?

Think about it very, very carefully... Look back and reflect on your past actions and decisions... Who and what do they typically benefit? We ALL serve something, whether it be our own desires or a noble cause, whether it be ourselves or a team. But the Call to Service is a recognition of committing ourselves to serve something greater than ourselves.

Have you answered that call?

THE BAR OF STANDARDS

How do we measure achievement? When do we know that we have achieved success in life? How do we measure the value and worth of success? There seem to be many people out there who claim to have the answers to these types of questions, and yet far greater a number quickly ready to discredit any who dare suggest a standard too high for social acceptance... And I'll tell you why that is, but first, understand this: REAL success is a never-ending struggle, and the reason for that, is because it's a journey spent striving for the Out-of-Reach Bar, the Highest of Standards, the Bar forever just barely out of reach...

Real success in life is the act of continuously raising the Bar of Standards, striving to reach that bar, and when your fingers can just barely touch it, raising it again. Real success does not come easy nor cheap and most certainly isn't handed out in the streets. There exists zero liberalism or socialism in the achievement of success, for it is an endeavor that cannot be obtained, borrowed, or stolen and redistributed from someone else. It is an endeavor to which only the individual himself or herself is capable. Yet all too often do we find the vast majority inescapably incapable of its attainment. Why? It's simple; most quit before they have ever taken the first step.

You see, life is filled to the hilt with overflowing, unprecedented mediocrity and underachievement. We are unfortunate enough to live in a society where mediocrity is hailed and praised as "achievement", and to where real achievement is often ridiculed and shunned. A society where very few truly shine above the rest and accomplish great and meaningful things, all because they were the only ones willing to strive for them. And because the rest complain of the effort required to obtain greatness, society opts instead to lower the Bar of Standards down to their own mediocre levels, so they may praise themselves, pat themselves on the back, and tell themselves that their new substandard level of achievement was meaningful and worthwhile.

But such things are not worth praising! For if we do allow the praise of such willful underachievement, then an ever new "lowering of the standard" shall continuously become the next socially accepted subject of praise! Before you know it, there will be fewer and fewer of those willing to challenge the highest peaks or dive to the deepest of depths! Fewer and fewer of those willing to escape from the bubble, boldly tell society to its face that its standards are worthlessly low, and strive to reach real stars! Society will eventually be reduced to one that praises itself just for showing up, and hands itself a trophy merely for living and breathing and taking up space!

Oh, wait... it has already...

I'll tell you right here and now, such a low standard of achievement is worthless and meaningless, and unless the standard is moved to a place beyond your own reach, it isn't worth striving for. The vast majority are uncomfortable with the idea of being uncomfortable and dismissive of the need for discomfort as a requirement for success. But discomfort is at the heart of the journey to success, and unless individuals are willing to leave their lazy bubbles of comfortable mediocrity, their lives will never amount to anything worth anything worthy of praise.

Many might read this and shout aloud, "But, if the bar is set too high, we'll likely never reach it!" And to this I say, you lot of lazy demagogues, the bar should always be out of reach! If you ever reached the bar, would you not then cease to grow? Should you strive along your journey, leaving the comforts of your bubble behind, and reach the bar, would not your journey reach an end? For the true leader set-forth upon the road of self-betterment – the journey to success – a stagnant life is one not worth living! But if the bar is always and forever just out of reach, set higher and higher each time you get closer, you'll soon find you've reached unprecedented heights, and look back to marvel at all you've achieved! Such a journey is rightly truly worthy of praise!

Knowing this, there will surely still remain doubters, questioning, "But what's the first step? Certainly, it must be difficult for any who have never begun such a journey, what say you then?" And to them I say, for you relentless doubters who fallaciously demand more proof because you refuse to be moved and lack initiative, the first step shall always be the most difficult, and rightfully so, known by, "Responsibility" ...

The journey towards the achievement of success is a never-ending and difficult path of self-betterment – a path of leadership development – and it all starts with accepting responsibility for yourself and your own actions. Accept that your life is what you choose to make of it. Accept that no one can make your life better except you. Accept that no one is to blame for your life being what it is but you. Accept that nothing worth anything meaningful in life ever comes easy. And accept that without pain and hardship, sacrifice and struggle, difficulty and failure, you will never learn, you will never grow, and you will never achieve.

Real success requires you to accept responsibility for yourself, and then take action to make a positive change. It requires you to hold yourself accountable and take the initiative to do what needs to be done, to focus on reaching that Out-of-Reach Bar. The world isn't at fault for your shortcomings and lot in life, you are! Don't blame others for your faults and failures, or problems you help create... Instead, take a look at yourself for once, commit to the goal, hold yourself accountable, focus on personal change, and keep moving forward. But remember, that once you commit to the journey, that overwhelming majority of society, the same majority hell-bent on lazy stagnation, will shun you and even curse you once they realize you will not do the hard work for them. They will hate you for your success because they envy you and what you've earned and despise themselves for not doing the same.

No, real success is not easy, it cannot be bought, borrowed or taken, and it comes at a steep personal price. It requires complete acceptance of personal responsibility and accountability and a serious commitment to the journey. You must commit your life to discomfort, to struggle and pain, and through it all, commit to having the backbone and the fortitude to walk your journey for yet another day. To cast aside your weak feelings of pity and pessimism... To the deep-sixing of dead weight and developing an iron will. Real success isn't for everyone – as history has shown, society doesn't like it when everyone can't be winners. Society will scream at you that you're wrong, that you should remain weak just like them, and that you should freely give away the merit of your own hard work to those who've done nothing, achieved nothing, and amounted to nothing... But real success is an achievement attained only by leaders – those initiative-takers, those trend-setters – those who never stop reaching for the Out-of-Reach Bar, the one held to the Highest of Standards, the Bar forever just barely out of reach...

So today... Take a cold hard look at your life with all seriousness, accept real responsibility, honestly hold yourself fully accountable in the gaze at that reflection, and ask yourself if you have yet to cast aside the comfortable bubble of mediocrity and take that first step! Decide for yourself if you're strong enough to take up such an endeavor, and if so, commit! Raise your Bar of Standards to great heights well beyond your grasp and strive daily toward reaching it! And when you've gotten close, when your fingers draw near and you're finally just barely able to touch the bar... Raise your standards once again! Before long, you'll be able to turn back, look down the sides of that Mountain with No Summit, and marvel at how far you've gone. If anything, knowing there's no end in sight, seeing all you've achieved through your efforts thus far should provide more motivation to keep you going...

After all, a stagnant life is one not worth living, and the only one capable of reaching your dreams... Is you.

DOUBT

What makes you think for one second that you CAN'T do something? That you can't achieve your goals? That you can't make the distance? That you won't measure up? Just stop and think about that for a second... You've trained hard, you spent time learning everything there is to know, you improved your knowledge, skills, and abilities, and now you're finally ready to put yourself to the test... You know very well that you're capable. You've been through far more difficult things in the past, right? You've prepared for this moment set before you, and now it's your time to shine... So, what's holding you back from being successful?!

I'll tell you what it is... It's "doubt".

"Doubt" is a disease of the mind, and it will rob you of your chances for victory without you ever realizing it. It will prevent you from staying the course, from keeping positive, from pushing through the pain and discomfort, and from ever being successful. Doubt will creep up on you, consume your thoughts, your motivation, and your willpower, and it will leave you weak, exhausted, and self-defeated in agony.

Remember when we talked about "beating yourself" back on Day 13? If you were a well-prepared marathon runner, doubt is the only thing that will prevent you from finishing the race. If you were a mountain climber, self-doubt is the one thing that will keep you from scaling the highest peaks. If you were a speed swimmer, doubt is the one thing that will keep you from being competitive. Doubt in your mind over your ability to achieve, to succeed, and to make the goal, will stop you from rising to the challenge, accepting increased levels of responsibility, ruin your chances for promotion, destroy your ability to lead, and could even get you killed should your life depend on your ability to be successful in your endeavor.

Remember when we discussed how our minds will quit on us long before our bodies will? Well... If more people understood how something so small as the whisper of doubt poisons our thoughts and robs us of our internal motivation, we'd see far more remarkable achievements throughout our lifetimes. If people only understood how self-doubt can make a successful entrepreneur quit, crumble an organization from within, prevent the most qualified from getting the job, put a Soldier's life in jeopardy, and ruin a great leaders ability to lead, then we'd see far more amazing ideas come to fruition, far more great businesses growing the economy, far more of the brightest in the highest positions, and far more amazing individuals rising to the occasion, growing those around them, and accomplishing great and meaningful things.

Today, take time to reflect on all those times you worked hard for something but weren't successful, those times you quit before you tried, when you made an excuse for not showing up... Think of those times in your life when you stayed quiet instead of speaking up, when you didn't volunteer but thought you should have, or when you questioned your ability to win the race, reach the goal, or achieve a success... You know what kept you from trying and succeeding? You doubted yourself. We've all done it, but it's now time to put an end to that. Now's the time to believe in yourself more than ever. Tell yourself you can, and you will! Then go get it done!

Your journey to success has already begun... Do you doubt you can make it? You just have to truly believe you can do it... That's all it takes.

HAVE A "CAN DO" ATTITUDE

Go ahead... Tell me you can't make it! Tell me you're incapable! Argue with me that "no one ever has"! Mention how "that's the way it's always been"! Blame someone or something else, cry it's all their fault, and attempt to justify to me your pessimism! Shoot the possibility down as impossible, the idea as improbable, and the obstacles impassable! Give me every weak-minded, weak-willed, pathetic, cowardly, self-defeatist excuse you can think of...

Because we like knowing who's truly worth our time, and who's not.

Regardless if as an individual, or as a member of a team, being sober of mind and honest about the realities of a situation is never wrong, and in fact, teammates being willing to admit up front what we're facing has saved my life, and the lives of others, many times in the past... But a diatribe is no friend to a team, and pessimism is no friend to success. In our most desperate hour of need, where the rubber meets the road, a "can do" attitude and a smile on your face can and will make all the difference between coming out the other end or not at all...

Now don't get it twisted here! I NEVER said it would be easy! I NEVER said you wouldn't get a few scrapes or scars along the way either... In fact, I KNOW I've preached countless times that it WILL be hard, and I've proclaimed to that fact how the difficulty of the journey is the very reason the journey itself is worth it! The harder you work to reach the other side, the more meaningful the reward shall be! If you want to reach the stars, you have to be willing to climb the mountain...

Make no mistake about it, you're in the interview of your life on a daily basis. Welcome to Selection! The goal here is to purposely weed out the non-hackers and see who's left standing! I got news for you... Life doesn't care if NO ONE makes it through Selection! So, there are no tears shed for those who got dismissed early or didn't make it in the end. The "Team of Success" isn't looking for just "everyone" to join. There are no "inclusion initiatives", zero need for "diversity", and no "affirmative action policies" here... The team striving for exceptionalism, for achieving real success, doesn't care who you are, what minority group or self-victimhood group you claim... NO ONE is guaranteed a spot. They want only one thing... And that's the "right person for the right job". They want the one who won't quit, who won't give up, who – come hell or high water, and no matter the odds – will FIND a way to succeed. They want that "Can Do" attitude!

THAT's who the team is looking for!

So, go ahead and give me all your excuses! Tell me you don't think you can make it... Because if you're the type of person who defeats yourself before the journey has even begun... Then you might as well stay put in the valley, keep dreaming, and be just as mediocre as everyone else... If you aren't willing to put forth the effort to rise to the occasion, we don't want you on this mountain-climbing team, period. You're interviewing for your spot every day! And if selected, you have to earn the right to keep your spot every single day too!

Today... Think long and hard if you're willing to sacrifice it all so that the team – AND YOURSELF – will achieve success... The journey to success is waiting, and your selection process has already begun... Will you make the cut?

SUCCESS IS EARNED

Here's the bottom line up-front... There exists zero socialism in success.

Yes, you read that right, and yes, that word was specifically chosen to make a point you must learn here and now if you're ever going to grow and achieve... Success is something that must be EARNED. It doesn't come easy or cheap. It can't be bought, borrowed, given, or stolen either. The reason that word is being used here is because far too many have been brainwashed to believe in impossible utopian ideals of obtaining something for nothing.

No, you can't steal the merit of someone else's hard work and redistribute it to yourself and others. "Success" isn't something so tangible and quantifiable that it's easily stripped of those who've earned it. It can't be legislated to be taken away, nor can it be taxed. Just because you haven't attained a measure of it doesn't give you any right to the success someone else has created, and starting off life with more in no way automatically means you had it from the beginning... That would be an assumption that material possessions and wealth are THE physical forms of "success". This isn't true at all, and it brings us to the next point...

There's no equity in success either as it's not possible to manufacture the creation of success. You don't get a leg-up or a head start just because you choose to claim some form of victimhood and blame society for your lot in life. You don't get freebies at the expense of those who've worked hard just because you cry that life isn't fair. Guess what? It's not. Plain and simple, life isn't fair. It never has been, and never will be, and the sooner you get over yourself and accept that fact, the sooner you can begin earning your way toward achieving your OWN success in life...

The reason why it doesn't matter if you're rich or poor, born into luxury or poverty, that you can't force the redistribution of "success" by stealing it from those who have it and giving it to those who haven't earned it, is because it's not tangible. Success is a lot of things, and it has no set-in-stone definition, but there is an outlining to its aspects. It is plainly understood as one thing... The reward for hard work and achievement... To each person that means something a little different and a little alike. One person may claim to start a business or to be climbing the corporate ladder and amassing wealth equals success, but it isn't... While the wealth is the fruit of their labor, the reward of their hard work is the satisfaction of a job well done, and that's the measure of success they have gained along the way. Another person may claim owning a home and raising a family through college equals success, but it isn't... It's the joy of seeing the family grow and flourish, of imparting life-lessons that prepare children for the REAL world, and seeing them work hard to achieve their own success that is the measure of success they have gained along the way... Both these examples have different tangible gains, but both have the same understanding that the success gained in their endeavors were earned through the merit of their own hard work.

Today, contemplate carefully the meaning of "success", and the price that must be paid to obtain it. You need to understand that it's your responsibility to bring success to your life. It's not your neighbors, not society's, not the wealthy, nor is it the government's job to make you successful, it's yours. And until you stop blaming everyone and everything else, and start looking in the mirror, taking personal responsibility, holding yourself honestly accountable, and begin focusing on striving for self-betterment, you'll NEVER amount to anything. The sooner you learn that, understand that, and willingly admit that, the sooner you can finally begin to climb the mountain for yourself. And the sooner you start your own journey, the sooner you will finally begin to realize the success you dream of.

BE. KNOW. DO.

At the end of the day, striving toward continuous personal improvement and self-betterment ultimately results in developing your potential as a leader. Leaders are not born, despite the contentions of those determined to suggest some are, no... Leaders are "made". They are made through the progression of a purposeful and willful pursuit striving toward personal development. They are forged by the very journey you've embarked upon. The trials, challenges, hardships, and adversities you'll face along the way have the potential to become crippling and agonizing stumbling blocks of defeat, or they can become building blocks of strength and opportunity that shape you into a person of great character capable of leading the way toward achieving success, and showing others how to get there.

By taking up the journey, you'll begin leading intrinsically by example, you'll gain the necessary knowledge and wisdom required to be effective in your actions, and as a result, know what works, what doesn't, and how to pass that knowledge on to others... And THAT is why right now is the perfect time to discuss and understand the "Be. Know. Do." Philosophy of Leadership. "Be. Know. Do." is short for "Character, Knowledge, and Action".

When we talk about what leaders "are", leaders are THE embodiment of "being" the example. They are the shining examples of what "right" looks like. They are the standard-bearers and the guideposts, and even if they aren't involved directly in leading others, their actions taken along their own journey sets an example others can follow – thus leadership is possible even with no one to lead...

So BE the example. Understand your values and attributes and let them positively and constructively grow your confidence. KNOW your job, yourself, your team, and focus on continued learning. Your competence includes everything from technical skills to people skills, understanding your limitations, the needs of others, and accepting that learning is a life-long process. And DO your job, your part, and the right thing at all times. Your actions speak louder than your words and doing your job without complaint, meeting your part of the teams' needs, and even the way you treat others, all speak volumes about what kind of leader you are. Whether you're a good leader or a toxic waste can be seen by everyone in the way you act and what you do.

'Be, Know, Do' is short but powerful as a leadership philosophy because it covers the entire definition of leadership – including values and personal development; conceptual, interpersonal and technical skills; and operating, influencing, and improving. It's the total encompassment of the self; three broad areas that cover nearly every aspect of your potential, and if focused on developing over time, will ultimately craft a well-rounded character.

Therefore, today is a day to focus on how well-rounded your personal development might be and consider carefully how your own leadership philosophy may or may not have helped to guide that development. If you find that maybe your personal philosophy of the past hasn't been the most helpful, consider your future goals and making adjustments to help you reach them – or even consider adopting a new leadership philosophy altogether. BE the example, KNOW what needs to be done, and DO the right thing, and you'll lead the way up the mountain toward achieving success.

CORE DEVELOPMENT DAYS

THE JOURNEY BEGINS

Just beyond the horizon rests a mountain of opportunity, ready and waiting for you to show up and accept its challenges. Yet to reach that mountain, you must cross a sea of adversity.

Indeed, we all begin our journey in life standing at the shore of a vast sea, staring out into the distance, at a far-off mountain seemingly endless in height, having no summit in sight, whereupon our hopes and dreams may be found. Yet to reach them, you have to cross the sea, brave the storms, tread the valley, climb the mountain, and overcome all the hardships along the way. We have a choice to make... Do we embark upon the journey to cross the sea, to reach and climb the mountain, and strive to achieve success? Or do we decide the effort required isn't worth it and stay put on that beach, spending our lives merely dreaming of all the possibilities that could be?

Well, this is not a story of a stagnant life... No... This is a story – your story – of taking the journey, growing, and achieving success, and the moral of the story here, is that success in life is only possible through our own hard work, and opportunities to reach that success exist within the very challenges, hardships, trials, and adversities bound to occur along the way.

Great rewards can be found at the summit of our hard work and efforts, and the knowledge and wisdom we gain by enduring the hardships of the journey, forge our character and can strengthen our resolve. Yet most people will never take the journey to climb that far-off mountain because all they see is how far away it is, the magnitude of the efforts required to reach it, and an ocean at their feet. Most people look at trial and adversity, challenges and hardships, only as that... Trial and adversity, challenges and hardships, and they scorn the idea of them. Successful people, on the other hand, see those things as opportunities for success and face them, are thankful for them, praise them, and embrace them for the blessings and growth they provide.

Successful people use the knowledge and wisdom gained from their journey, and the strength of character and intestinal fortitude developed within them from the trials and adversities encountered along the way, to achieve great and meaningful things with their lives. They don't cower away from the sight of adversity coming their way, hoping they can weather the storms and ride out the waves to somehow make it through to the other side and live to see another day... No... They prepare for them, plan for them, face them head on while looking them in the eyes, and learn from them so they can grow and reach their goals!

So, today's the day! You're standing on that beach, staring across the expanse, and seeing your dreams across the way... The thrill of LIFE and adventure is resonating deep within you, beckoning for you to answer the call and embark upon your journey! You've built your foundation, you know who you are, and what you stand for. You've acknowledged that you are your greatest obstacle and that your attitude makes all the difference. You've reconciled with past choices and quit making excuses... NOW is the time to finally take the first step into the water...

The journey is before you.

Are you ready, willing, and able to take it?

LIFE IS A SERIES OF STORMS

Do you know what Aviators, SCUBA Divers, Special Operations Operators, Firefighters, and even Astronauts all have in common? These individuals don't deal with risk by "hoping" they'll survive and make it through... No, they mitigate risk through careful planning, and backup planning, and planning backups to their backup's... They study every aspect and angle and are experts at becoming experts. They train and stay motivated to a purpose... So that when the time comes to put their skills to the test, they are competent and confident, and willingly face challenges head-on. They don't cower before the storm and "hope" they make it out the other side alive... They study, prepare, train, and boldly face it head-on, and come out the other end with a smile on their face! And if, by some chance, they don't make it, history remembers them for their greatness in the face of great odds.

So let's get an understanding here... Understand that the very second you stepped off that beach and ventured out into the open seas, the very second you committed and embarked on your journey, you accepted the fact that you're going to encounter storms great and small along the way. That's life, that's reality, and that fact is something beyond your control. So, accept it, and instead of crying about it, focus on the things that you CAN control – like planning and preparing for them – then look forward to facing them when they come... And make no mistake, they are already on the way...

This was said before, on Day 1 no less, that the fact of the matter is, life doesn't CARE about YOU, and being "successful" at life is hard. Life is like a series of storms, it's wild, unpredictable, and turbulent, and it will destroy you with a smile. One second you could be basking in the sun, taking it easy and enjoying the good times, then in the next moment, you could be slammed by the waves, high winds bearing down upon you, thrown about and pounded by heavy rains.

Life doesn't care if you're weak, it doesn't care if you've had no sleep, it couldn't care less if you're unprepared, tired, and ready to quit. No, you're not special, your feelings don't matter, and suggesting it isn't fair and crying about it all won't stop it either... One after the next the storms WILL come, and what matters MOST in life, is NOT whether you've survived the storms, it's how you chose to face them when they came. And it is THAT... That right there, is ultimately what determines both how we grow and develop as a person and a leader, and how history will remember us long after we're gone.

That moment is the singular most defining moment of our lives... That moment in how we chose to face life's storms...

Today, consider this thought... Human beings have a remarkable ability to become truly exceptional in the face of great trial and grow the most in the shadow of hardship. Then ask yourself, how will you choose to face the storms you'll encounter on the open seas now that you've embarked upon your journey? Are you learning, training, and preparing? Or do you expect to make it through each time on the idea of "hope"? Or will you cower in the face of them as they bring the sheer wrath of God down upon you? Make your choice, and choose wisely, because you can't choose your consequences. You may not have a choice in the fact that trials and hardship will come your way, but you do have a choice in how you face those things when they happen.

YOU CAN'T ROW YOUR BOAT ALONE

Leaving the beach, making your passage through the surf and out into the open ocean, and sailing your way across the expanse successfully, greatly depends on how well those with you can work together as a team. The reality of taking your journey is that there's no way you'll ever make through your own efforts alone... You will need the help of a team to achieve success along the way.

But, of course, nothing is ever as simple as that, now is it? After all, simply gathering a bunch of people together and handing them ores, telling them to push a boat in the water and row together, isn't going to make them a "team". Teams need to come together and see themselves as members of the team, as partners in a collective effort, and it is that shared consciousness that becomes the driving force behind teamwork.

Teamwork implies the willingness, preparedness, and proclivity of each individual member of the team to back fellow members up during operations. Good teams are distinguishable from bad teams in that their members show a willingness to jump in and help out when needed, and they willingly accept help from each other. After all, teamwork is a dynamic process that requires all members to pull their own weight while looking out for each other. For teamwork to be effective, group members must collectively view themselves as a group whose success depends on collective interaction. Team members must have a high awareness of themselves as a team, and each member should see the team's success as taking precedence over individual performance. Therefore, members of effective teams view themselves as connected team members, not as isolated individuals simply working with other isolated individuals. The teams' success equals their success, and the teams' failure, their failure...

There's a reason why organizations are made up of teams and not merely individuals... Many hands make light work, many eyes keep everyone safe, but teamwork is only effective if those on the team are motivated to strive for the collective effort. Yes, individuality is important. People need to know it matters who they are as a person. But when it comes to accomplishing the mission, thinking only of yourself will quickly put the mission and everyone around you at risk. Solid team-building means setting personal matters aside and focusing on collectivity. When it's time to be a part of a team, it's time to put the needs of the many before your own. So, let's face it... At the end of the day, you can't row your boat alone, you'll never break the surf.

Today, consider this... Up until now, your journey has largely been about working on developing yourself from within, and preparing yourself for embarkation... And while that's still the case, now it's time to admit you need help if you're ever going to cross the sea... You will require the assistance of many teams if you're ever going to make progress along your journey, and good leadership involves knowing how to develop teamwork while fostering a team atmosphere. Your teams will never reach the goal if all you have is a bunch of individuals focused solely on their own tasks, or individuals that are members of the team, but who are constantly excluded from the dynamic. Successful teams depend on each other, and it's YOUR job as the leader to grow mutuality of concern within your team. Get them rowing together while helping each other out! Get them to see themselves as one, and that the team's success equals their success! Otherwise... You'll end up dumped back on the beach by the waves... Right back where you started from.

OPEN OCEAN SWIMS

The open ocean is a desert of water, void of diverse terrain, and without activities and opportunities for recreation and relaxation along the way, your team's motivation to press on will quickly begin to fade. Thus, "swim call" is a timeless activity sailors the world-over have enjoyed as a means of refreshing themselves – physically and mentally – from the daily grind... Yet preparing to jump ship and swim out into the open ocean can be daunting for some. It is an exercise in both courage and humility, as well as an act of dedication and willpower, to say the least.

On one hand, the depths of the sea invite a presence of the unknown into your mind, and many are fearful of what might lurk in the depths that they cannot see. While on the other hand, you must realize before you ever step foot off the boat and leap into the water, that should you venture out, you'll still have to overcome the seas mighty forces in order to make it back alive. Thus, you must remain dedicated to the task, and have the endurance to survive the journey. The power of the sea should force a level of respect upon you to take it seriously, lest you succumb to its tow and perish.

Much is the same with our journey through life. You must have the courage to face life's unknowns, the humility to respect what is more powerful than yourself, remain dedicated to your path and the commitments you've made, and the strength to endure. These four character traits are essential keys to your personal development and growth as you sail the open seas, and later, they will become hallmarks of your effectiveness as a leader whom others deem worth following.

Life is undoubtedly filled with lurking predators and unknown dangers. It's natural to be afraid of the possibility of encountering these things, but courage is the ability to take action despite our fear. Knowing full-well the forces of nature are more powerful than ourselves, if we ever want to play in nature's playground and survive, we must respect it. Having respect for something means we make a real effort to learn about it, understand it and how it can impact us, and treat it with caution... But having respect for something we intend to engage with also means we take the time to prepare ourselves for that interaction. We learn to swim in this case, we train, develop and refine our technique, and build our endurance – which leads to building confidence as well. Using our courage and respect, and having prepared, we take the plunge and commit to our decision, and see it through to make it back safe and sound.

Even in our down time, in our quest for relaxation while venturing along our journey for success, opportunities for self-betterment will present themselves. How we choose to take advantage of those opportunities or not can and will go a long way toward determining the type of person we'll end up as by the time we reach the mountain waiting for us on the other side. Today, take some time to consider possible missed opportunities for growth in your past. Have you participated in activities similar to a Sailor's "swim call"? Or did you pass, say "no thanks", and remain on the sidelines as you watched everyone else muster up their courage and take the plunge? If so, now's the time to make a personal commitment never to repeat that mistake again.

A SEA OF POSSIBILITIES

In life, we are a ship in an endless Sea of Possibilities, threatened by raging Storms of Adversity, guided by a navigator called Choices, kept afloat by the forces of Faith and Motivation, and measured by a unit known as Character.

Life – the fact of the matter is – doesn't really care about us, and the Storms of Adversity will slam into us, and threaten us, redirect our bearings, and capsize us given the opportunity, time, and time again. Yet should we accept survivals challenges, put forth our best efforts, rise to the occasion, and face adversity head-on, boundless possibilities shall reveal themselves, and to our advantages, the benefits shall become our sweet reward.

What matters MOST in life, is NOT whether or not we manage to survive life's storms... No... What matters most in life, is how we choose to face them when they come. That choice will go on to have lasting impacts throughout the rest of our lives. It will determine whether we'll end up a coward stagnating in the valley later on, or a great leader of courageous character boldly climbing the mountain... It will also determine how history remembers us long after we're gone.

Understand this... Adversity is quite possibly life's greatest teacher. If you'd only listen, you'd hear some of the wisest words in existence... That EVERY hardship is a lesson, and every setback an opportunity... That the ONLY thing that will EVER keep YOU from success is YOU. If you chose to see life's adversities as beasts of burden, that pessimism will most assuredly guarantee you'll never amount to anything. Yet, if you're able to hunt the good stuff, find the silver linings, stay positive and optimistic, and with a bit of tenacity smile and tell life's adversities to "do their worst" ... You'll more clearly be able to find opportunities within those events to grow, to win, to achieve and succeed, and come out on top – if ANYTHING, a better, stronger, wiser person than you were going in.

Don't misunderstand here... bad events happen throughout our lives, and it sucks! It truly does! But the real lesson here is that you have a choice in how you decide to handle those events beyond your control, and at THIS point in your journey, you should already be WELL-beyond that "woe is me" mentality!

So, stand tall and face life's storms with courage, Faith in your heart, and humility, that you may learn and grow and become stronger and wiser from them! And on the other side... Bask in the warmth, beauty, and glory, of a new day - and new adventures - rising above the horizon, greeting you on the other side. Today's a day to reflect on the many storms you've weathered thus far... Did you make it here on the winds of dumb luck? Or are you alive and kicking today due to facing them head-on, learning and growing with each, till now you can sail through them with skill? If you're here merely by God's good graces, perhaps now's your chance to change your character, grow a spine, and learn to face your problems. There is a Sea of Possibilities filled with opportunities before you... You only need to learn to see it that way to take advantage of them.

How you chose to face those moments that test you is what matters most because the content of your character will ultimately become the key to your success, or the linchpin of your demise.

LISTEN TO YOUR PEOPLE

We all have two eyes, and two ears, but only one mouth... Now THERE'S a classic we've all heard as kids... But there's real wisdom in those words. Many people are quick to speak, but not so quick to watch, listen, learn, or seek to understand.

Far too often people hear only to respond, instead of listening to truly understand each other. When engaged in conversation, or a disagreement, many are so anchored in their own position that they never seek to understand the other side, but instead only ever wait for their turn to respond with their own opinions, positions, and/or biases. This attitude often has its roots in pride, and in the realm of leadership, arrogant pride will quickly become a toxic venom that destroys an organization from within. Absolutely, you may be very smart, but refusing to listen to others due to the mistaken belief that they can't teach you anything isn't smart at all. It's a highly unintelligent attitude that only works instead to create division and friction, which in turn, ruins morale, disrupts capabilities, and eats away at mutuality of concern.

Every member that has earned their place on your team has something they can teach you, an idea to bring to the table, and some wisdom they can impart. Instead of simply hearing their words while waiting for your chance to respond, you should be listening carefully to what they say so you can understand their message and possibly learn something new. According to I/O Psychology, each member of your team is a qualified Subject-Matter Expert (SME) in their job(s), and as such, they are your best source of information. You may have a plan, but they may have an idea for how to accomplish the mission that's more effective or efficient than the one you thought of. There may be a disagreement, but if you listen to understand the other side, you may find a better solution, or perhaps you might discover you're both on the same side but have merely been expressing yourselves from different perspectives.

Remember this... Leadership as a process isn't restricted to simplistic vertical chain-of-command structures, but instead works laterally across an organization, and this means it has no restrictions to influence. Anyone can be a leader at any level within an organization, at any time, and this means every member of the team has equal capability to influence and bring value to the organization.

Today, consider your ability to use your ears twice as much as your mouth. Everyone has something to bring to the table, and everyone is capable of exerting leadership influence regardless of where they stand on the team. Refusing to allow yourself to be influenced by someone simply because of their rank, status, or position, not only isn't very intelligent, but the toxicity of such an elitist attitude can and will quickly turn your team against you. Real leadership is a never-ending process of self-betterment, and that means everyone is capable of it.

What's the lesson here? Listen to your people... You might learn something.

BUILD MUTUALITY OF CONCERN

We all know camaraderie is what makes or breaks your experience in any group, and it can also become the essential component required for the group to achieve success, but if that relationship is true, then what exactly leads to building camaraderie?

When people decide to join a group, organization, or become a member of a team, they usually assume that those group members they will be working with share the same level of commitment, maintain the same values, and generally hold many of the same ideals as they do. However, the truth is that everyone brings a unique perspective and their own set of skills and experiences to the group, and that also means that not everyone in the group will initially maintain the same levels, values, or ideals as others do. This is why it is so important for leaders to work hard towards establishing mutuality of concern as early as possible.

What is mutuality of concern? It's the degree to which members of a team share the same level of commitment to the team. Simply put, mutuality of concern is the idea that members of the same group each individually share in similar levels of commitment for the group, its goals, the mission, etc., and that each member has independently internalized that commitment as a form of personal responsibility. When most or all of the group members share high levels of mutuality of concern, the group is more successful, but when personal goals and individualist behaviors conflict with the group's goals, the results are counterproductive. As such, we can establish a clear relationship between group success and the internalized level of commitment maintained by each member of the group.

Individuals initially enter a group with different levels of commitment based primarily on their current understanding of the nature of the group, their initial interactions with the other group members, how those things relate to their own past experiences, and their initial motivations for joining the group in the first place. Unfortunately, this also means that there may be individuals who couldn't care less about the group or its mission, but instead see it as an opportunity to further their own self-interests. These individuals maintain little to no mutuality of concern for the group, its members, or its mission because their own hidden agenda(s) and selfish individualistic attitude(s) takes priority in their own minds. A hidden agenda is a private goal in which an individual(s) work toward while seemingly working toward the team's goal(s). It would not be an understatement then to suggest that hidden agendas can also become the ultimate downfall of a team, lead to mission failure, and destroy the organization as a whole from within.

So how can we help to avoid such things? For starters, it is very important to establish early on a clear definition of the level of commitment required for the group to succeed – considering the group's agenda and its goals – and then communicating that definition to all group members. This should be followed up by getting feedback from each member of the group to understand the level of commitment each member currently has. Essentially, it is imperative to clearly understand the degree to which each member is concerned with the group's mission from the beginning, and that means getting all group members to clearly state their level of personal commitment to the group, their needs while a member of the group and their goals both personal and professional.

The key for leaders is to establish whether or not a member's stated level of personal commitment matches the defined level previously established. If not, why not, and is there anything that can be done to improve it? Next, understanding each person's individual needs allows leaders and other group members to help meet those needs. Part of a leader's inherent responsibility of being a leader is the Stewardship of Leadership itself, and that means helping those who support you grow and develop themselves so they can achieve their own desired goals. And finally, knowing what individual goals a person maintains allows leaders to establish whether or not that individual might help the group or hinder it. For those individuals whose personal goals do not line up with the goals required by the group, leaders might question those individual's level of commitment, their desire to be a member of the group, whether or not they possibly maintain any hidden agendas, and whether or not they should be a part of the team.

Finally, all team members should hold each other to a set standard of accountability and align that standard to the previously expressed definition of required commitment. Accountability is important. Not only is this an area where leadership stands a great opportunity to generate motivation, highlight achievement, and build esprit de corps, but at the same time, without accountability, some individuals might attempt to skate by while others do all the work. Social loafing – the tendency for some individuals to hold back from contributing (to loaf) in a team because they assume someone else will do the work – is a major hindrance to the establishment, growth, and internalization of mutuality of concern, and holding each other accountable is the best way to combat this type of behavior.

Today's a day to reflect very carefully on your own personal degree of Mutuality of Concern. Start by honestly considering if your own personal interests align with the mission and goals of the team and organization you belong to. Does your own intended level of commitment match theirs? If you find your own interests don't exactly line up, consider this... Do you maintain any problems, issues, or concerns that might prevent them from aligning with the goals of the group? Consider the standards set upon you... Do you hold yourself fully accountable to meet them?

The majority of people who want to be a member of a team typically have a high degree of mutuality of concern for the team because the team's success is their success. Establishing clear expectations, taking real concern for other group members, and holding people accountable will not only greatly improve your chances of fending off hidden agendas and social loafing, but it will also greatly improve the group's ability to develop a strong sense of mutuality of concern required to achieve success.

COMMUNICATION APPREHENSION

Bottom line up front... Communication is just as essential for teamwork as it is for your own individual success.

Our personally held preferences in our communication to others are an important and integrated part of our intrapersonal experiences with other people. How we relate to each other when speaking in conversation, how we talk to those within our inner circles and to those outside of those circles, as well as how we communicate to small and large groups and across entire organizations, are all a part of our own communicational predispositions. Each of these exchanges are impacted by our ability to choose the right form of communication, as well as our capacity and capability to communicate effectively with others in the process, but they also have a direct relationship with our personal preferences across other areas too... Everything from the choice of occupation, determination of job satisfaction, level of productivity, opportunities for advancement, desire for job retention, and most importantly of all, our leadership potential and capabilities, are greatly impacted by our ability to communicate. It is safe to assume then, that communicational predispositions and preferences not only influence behavior but also are an important part of our individual success.

Not everyone, however, finds it easy to communicate effectively with others, with their team, or across the organizational expanse...

Communication Apprehension is a predisposition for behavior described as an individual's level of fear or anxiety associated with either real or anticipated communication with others, and it can become the internalized killer of potential leadership development – and career progression as a result. Essentially, some individuals with lower levels of organizational communication competency may develop an apprehension predisposition towards attempting to communicate with others, and as such, they often end up spending less time interacting within the organization than others do, unable to confront problems and organizational issues, and even unable to express and/or address personal and professional issues or desires. Such apprehensions cause them to shy away from personal and professional opportunities due to fear or nervousness to organizational communicational requirements attached to those opportunities. This failure to develop, progress, and ultimately advance can become the downfall of personally perceived success, or even the killer of an otherwise successful career.

Today's a day to think about your own communication apprehension and predispositions. Has there ever been a time in your life when you knew something wasn't right, but you didn't say anything for even the slightest fear of not being received well by peers, a group or team, or even your leadership? Have you ever missed an opportunity because you failed to express your desire to go after it? Have you ever had an idea for a better, more effective method to accomplish a task, but didn't bring it up for some reason? Your team won't be successful if members don't feel they are able to communicate with each other, if one or more members seem unapproachable, or if team members are apprehensive about communicating, and you won't grow and achieve success in your own endeavors if you can't learn to speak up when you know you should. Every person alive has experienced communication apprehension at some point in their lives... What's important here, is to recognize it, so when you encounter it again, you can overcome that barrier, and grow.

EFFECTIVE COMMUNICATION

Our communication capability works just like a tower does... The higher in elevation you can get, the farther you can send your message... But so too does our capacity for communication find an equal comparison, since where you both design and place your tower ultimately determines its effectiveness at sending your message.

Many people seem to mistakenly believe that simply climbing the social and professional ladders automatically translates to a larger audience they can reach, and while this may seem true when looking at numbers, your communicational reach ultimately has much more to do its effectiveness at reaching active listeners willing to engage with your message than it does with your potential audience size and range alone.

You can have all the range in the world, but if your signal isn't clear, your message won't be received. You can have the loudest voice of all, but if you're not a respected, well-educated, intelligent, and reasoned voice, no one will listen. You can have a captive audience, but if you can't format your message appropriately, they won't understand it. Simply put, you can have the largest audience size in the world, but if all they do is "like" your message yet never take the time to listen to it nor take the time to understand it, your audience size is worthless... And at the same time... You can have an active and fully engaged audience, but if your message is incoherent, uninformed, uneducated, unintelligent, or otherwise irrelevant to that audience, it won't be effective, and it too will be just as worthless.

In order for your communication to be effective, you need reach and attention sure, but more importantly, you need the ability to send your message in a way the receiver can understand, and you need to reach people who WANT to understand. A tall platform from which to broadcast isn't all there is to communicating with others. You need to build the right tower, position it in the best possible place, and develop a clear message first before anyone will hear you, pay attention to you, and understand you.

Make no mistake about it... That "tower" is you. It's your position in the community, your standing amongst your peers, your platform socially and professionally... That tower is your life, and it grows higher and more effective the more you work to develop yourself.

Now that you've reflected on your willingness and desire to communicate – even if there's an instinctual apprehension to do so - today, take some time to consider how effective your communicational ability needs to be in order to reach those willing to listen. There's more to your ability to communicate than merely your title alone, and that's the point. So, as you build your personal tower, consider carefully how you grow yourself, where you choose to place yourself, who you're speaking to, and how you word your message. Be a tower that doesn't seek only height and reach, but quality placement and design as well, and your messages will be heard more clearly by more people and carry further than they did before.

LEARN TO ENGAGE IN
TOUGH CONVERSATION

We live in an era of emotionally weak, pathetically spineless people, where everything's watered down to cater to the lowest common denominator's worthless claims of offense and constitutional fragility. Instead of demanding those individuals better themselves, we shame the exceptional to appease the mediocre. Up front and honest... It's a sad fact. Political correctness and emotionally driven bias have divided and eroded our society's ability to confront and solve its own problems...

People today have been taught to avoid engaging in meaningful dialogue over subjects they feel emotional about or have strong convictions about. This has led to an avoidance of topics that span the spectrum of politics, religion, economics, social issues, and more, and the result has led to widespread ignorance and anti-intellectualism as a generalizable lack of understanding about those same topics, subjects, and issues has skyrocketed. In our age, people have been taught to ridicule and dismiss any thought, position, opinion, or fact that doesn't readily agree with their own thoughts, positions, and opinions. The result has created a society divided, and completely incapable of understanding and solving its own problems. Instead of listening to understand, people today dismiss anything that simply doesn't agree with their beliefs. Instead of seeking to learn facts, people frame them to fit their bias. This has created a society of echo-chambers, filled with fallacious arguments, incapable of critical thinking and intellectual discourse.

So why do I bring this up? What's the point here?

The point is... If you always let your emotions dictate for you what you think, speak, and how you act, you very likely have no real understanding of truth, and a very limited comprehension - if any - of facts. Making you highly likely to ignorantly attack anything you simply disagree with.

The problems we're experiencing across our society today are a compound of social conditioning from friends and family, bias indoctrination in educational institutions, unethical and immoral systematic agenda-driven propaganda attacks by the mass media, and technological advancements that are both highly addictive and strongly skew our perception of reality. Instead of allowing our own opinions and positions to be formed and changed by facts, we instead actively try to frame, cherry-pick, and manufacture a reality that agrees with our emotions and biases. Instead of accepting the world for what it really is and allowing it to shape our opinions, people ignore what they don't like and attack what doesn't agree with the messages in their echo chamber.

The reality exists that the vast majority of social problems – both at the individual level and across society – exist simply because one or both sides absolutely refuse to learn to willingly engage in dialogue in a meaningful way. People avoid conversations they disagree with, and as a result, we have a society filled to the hilt with individuals who are uneducated about the very topics they maintain strong opinions about. This ignorance grows over time, and as it grows, it leads to a vicious cycle of yet even more hardened bias and resistance to engage.

Today, take some time to seriously think about some of the difficult topics of conversation you have strong convictions about. Do you know beyond doubt that your convictions are founded in reality and facts? Do you engage in critical thinking – the willful seeking of alternative viewpoints and evidence counter to your own position, for the purpose of discovering whether your position is true or not, and allow your position to change if not? Do you cast your emotion, feelings, and bias, to the curb and willfully engage in well-reasoned discourse with others – listening to understand and not simply hearing to respond – in order to learn to solve problems?

If you can't answer these questions honestly or find that you maintain beliefs that prevent you from engaging in tough conversations over difficult topics... I got some bad news for you... You're part of the problem and now's just as good a time as any to focus on changing yourself, instead of trying to change others. I'm not suggesting that intellectual engagement in respectful, well-considered discourse will always be successful... If that were the case, the first half of this chapter wouldn't have been written. There's a lot of bias out there, and the vast majority of it exists out of ignorance. That ignorance creates a strong belief that people think they know something they don't, and because their lives are controlled by their emotions and not logic, reasoning, and critical thinking, there's no force on the planet that will ever convince them otherwise... The message here, however, is if you're ever going to make progress on your journey toward success in life, you can't be controlled by biased emotions. At some point, you have to learn to engage in those tough conversations about difficult topics and now's just as good a time as any.

GIVING DIRECTION

Gen. George S. Patton famously once said, "Never tell people how to do things. Tell them what to do and they will surprise you with their ingenuity."

As the captain of your vessel, boldly crossing the expanse before you, you'll quickly discover your attention nearly always divided between where you want to go and how you're going to get there. This inevitably means you'll be required to regularly task your people with duties and assignments that keep the ship moving forward and sailing true to your intended course. You can't be everywhere at once, and it's not possible for you to do every job required and man every station necessary to keep the ship sailing safely ahead, so what do you do?

You surround yourself with the best people possible to help you reach the goal, delegate authority, and then get out of the way and let people do what they do best...

It's part of the "Three D's" of leadership... Decide, Delegate, and Disappear...

Being a good leader has nothing to do with telling people how to do their jobs, but it does mean you'll be directly responsible for telling them what needs to get done. General Patton knew this. He understood fully that micromanagement wasn't leadership at all, it was merely bad management, and it did more than simply limit individual and organizational productivity, it fostered resentment, ruined morale, and crippled effectiveness. It also prevents the leader from remaining focused on their own responsibilities.

While you should have a well-developed understanding of each job aboard your ship, make no mistake about it, it's not your job to tell your people "how" to get things done... After all, if you have to tell a person how to do their job, you probably don't need that person doing that job in the first place, now do you? No, you don't. You might as well simply do the job yourself, and if that be the case, then what do you have people for in the first place? Your job is to assume responsibility for the big picture of things... The ship, your crew, and the mission... And that means you need to stay focused on those responsibilities and let the members of your crew handle theirs.

Leadership isn't management and providing people with direction is far more effective than telling them how to get the job done. So, for today, focus on understanding the difference between good leadership practices and bad management habits. Instead of telling people how to do things, focus on providing them with guidance and direction. Tell them what needs to happen, what you expect, what you need them to do for the team to be successful and let them go to work. Most people have a good understanding of how to accomplish the tasks that make up their jobs, and more often than not, they are fully capable of figuring out solutions to problems and coming up with creative ways to achieve the desired end result if you just let them.

Further, when people are held responsible for problem-solving their own tasks, a stronger sense of ownership and accountability grows within them. The accomplishment of difficult tasks builds confidence and morale increases with it. And before you know it, you'll have a capable and effective crew, competent and confident in their abilities and skills, and more ready and willing to look toward you for the direction and guidance needed for the team to reach the goal.

UNDERSTANDING MOTIVATION

By their very nature, all living creatures, human beings included, instinctually seek out to remain as comfortable as possible throughout life. To never hunger, never feel pain, to neither sweat nor shiver, to avoid loss or anger or sadness or remorse or regret, nor to be challenged beyond comfort physically or mentally... One might suggest the effort exhausted to remain as comfortable as possible, given uncomfortable conditions encountered, would qualify as a form of motivation that drives living things to take action and produce a favorable change leading back into their bubbles of comfortability... But they would be sadly mistaken. After all, we just established that this action is instinct, and as such, external factors or not, an action taken on instinct alone doesn't qualify as a form of motivation...

There are two kinds of motivation – External and Internal – but only one of the two qualifies as REAL motivation.

As the examples above point out, instinctual action taken as a response to factors external to ourselves is categorized as External Motivation. External motivation is driven by external factors that create discomfort. These are things like environmental conditions (such as temperature, climate, and changing weather conditions), physiological conditions (such as pain, fatigue, hunger body temperature, etc.), and psychological conditions (such as stress, emotional responses, suffering and dealing with consequences, and strong biases). External motivational factors typically act as strong stimuli of discomfort that prompt instinctual responses to make a change to regain a level or degree of comfort once again.

Examples can include (but are not limited to):

- If you're hot or cold, you add or take away clothing, or move to an area where the temperature is more desirable.
- If you're hungry or thirsty, you eat and drink.
- If you're tired or exhausted, you'll seek sleep or rest.
- If you're in physical pain, you'll actively seek to change the condition causing it or try to alleviate the pain.
- If you're in emotional or mental pain or distress, instinct will drive you to avoid whatever is causing those feelings.
- If you're angry or emotional, you'll act irrationally and may act out physically.
- If you have hardened biases or biases that exist out of ignorance, instinct will drive you to dismiss, ridicule or outright ignore any opposing view, positions, or facts that contradict your biases, or avoid anyone or anything that challenges them, creating an echo-chamber bubble of comfort for yourself.

External motivation is both temporary and fickle. The instinctual actions produced last only as long as it takes to reach a degree of comfort once again, and as external stimuli changes, so to do the actions taken, meaning there exists no consistency or integrity in motivational sources, only the act of self-preservation to a comfortable existence. Therefore, as you can guess, External Motivation is not "real" motivation at all, and as such, it is not the kind of motivation that you're now using to cross a vast sea, actively seeking self-betterment, on your journey to climb a mountain with no summit, achieve success, and reach your goals...

No... REAL motivation comes from within...

Internal Motivation is the only form of "real" motivation that exists, and despite all the leadership theory out there, all the developmental and self-help books marketed in your face, and all the professors and professional coaches that try to suggest otherwise, Internal Motivation is something that is virtually impossible to generate in other people. Internal motivation is derived by an extremely strong desire that grows from deep within a person, the seeds of which are planted when the individual fully accepts personal accountability and responsibility for their own lives and sees a real need for change and growth. This strong desire becomes rooted in the core of their very being, and it drives them to take actions to achieve things connected or related to that desire. These actions generate a strong sense of ownership – a personal investment and holding in the value of them – and the gains of which we see as justifying the expense we are guaranteed to encounter along the way... Discomfort.

That's right... Internal motivational factors produce actions contrary to our instinctual desire to remain comfortable, to leave our comfort behind us and seek out a specific goal in mind. They drive us to willingly endure pain and anguish, setbacks and frustration, hardship and adversity, to leave our comfort behind us, to become comfortable with being uncomfortable, so that we might engage in actively committing to and taking the journey to reach that goal. Internal motivation is lasting and enduring, strong and resilient, integral and unwavering. It is what pushes us to keep going despite being uncomfortable, to reach new heights, to tread new paths, to achieve new goals... To reach the stars. When two or more internally motivated people, driven toward a common goal, come together, a team is formed that is capable of remarkable feats. Sharing high degrees of commitment to the team itself and the mission at hand, a strong level of mutuality of concern grows, and the individuals become one unit capable of accomplishing great and meaningful things.

Today, take some time to identify and understand the motivational factors driving yourself and your team(s) to achieve success. External factors may produce temporary external actions, but they won't achieve lasting, meaningful results as the actions taken weren't derived from a source of REAL motivation. Sadly, you can't generate internal motivation within other people either, only within yourself. You can try to plant it, foster it, and nurture it once it exists, sure... But it's practically impossible to create it in people who have yet to establish that strong desire within themselves. You're acting on internal motivation right now in your journey toward self-betterment... And the only teams capable of helping you take that journey are those whose members are internally motivated themselves... Identify the source of your own internalized motivation, and find internally motivated members to fill your team with, and you'll be highly successful in your endeavor...

ACCOUNTABILITY AND RESPONSIBILITY

How often today, in our age, do we encounter a problem, see a mistake, find an error, or witness an issue unfold, to which the prevailing response is a witch hunt to point fingers, find someone at fault, and assign blame? When it comes to problems, issues, and mistakes, the prevailing attitude found throughout our society today is that someone or something else is always the "problem", always "at fault", and always "to blame". There's always someone or something that appears to be responsible for all our problems and everything wrong with the world and our lives...

From the smallest daily occurrence to the largest social issues, anything is subject to being blamed... Anything but ourselves, that is.

There's a theory out there, tell me if you know its name, and it goes like this, "All things being equal... The simplest explanation tends to be the right one..."

When faced with the reality that you failed at something, that you fell short, didn't measure up, didn't achieve the mark... only the ignorant and indoctrinated, heavily biased sheep confined to echo-chambers, participate in such finger-pointing blame game nonsense, and only mediocre anti-intellectual morons would suggest the whole world is responsible for the underachievement that exists in their own lives. Consider this...

Perhaps the "whole world" isn't really "to blame" for your life being what it is right now... Perhaps the ownership of that title really belongs to you! The messes and disasters, mistakes and woes of your life are yours and yours alone to own. You're not some pathetic victim of a mass conspiracy to keep you down or some socially manufactured systematic form of discrimination hell-bent on oppressing you... No. The only thing you're a victim of is your absolute refusal to accept personal responsibility for your life and hold yourself truly accountable for improving it.

Remember yesterday – Day 32 – when we talked about how personal acceptance of responsibility and accountability are some of the seeds from which an internalized desire to grow and achieve take root? Well, guess what, they are also powerful tools you can use to grow. They are the sails that allow you to sail against storm winds that blow you off the path, and the rudder that helps you stay on course.

Today, ask yourself... When was the last time you caught yourself hypocritically pointing a finger at someone else when you know you've done something similar? When was the last time you ignored the propaganda that tells you "everyone else" and "everything else" is to blame for your situation in life and simply looked at what you did (or didn't do) to cause it? When was the last time you stopped pointing fingers and simply focused on just being a better person yourself? Because if your answer isn't "yesterday" or "today" (considering the journey you're on right this moment) ... Perhaps that's something to think about...

If we want to make the world a better place, if we truly want to solve our most pressing social issues, and if we truly want to grow, achieve, and reach our dreams, we have to start with ourselves... We have to stop pointing fingers and start looking in the mirror. If we truly desire to be successful in our journey, we have to be internally motivated to personal development and growth, and that won't happen until we honestly accept full responsibility for our lives, our thoughts, our actions, and our failures and shortcomings, and begin holding ourselves accountable for a change. And I got news for you... You're halfway across the expanse of a bottomless ocean right now, where raging storms are steadily moving in to prevent your progress and send you sinking to the depths below...

There's no place left to hide, and nothing left to blame... If you've been simply faking it this far, you'll soon be in for a rude awakening.

— Day 34 —

LEARN "HOW" TO THINK

The sea offers the world air to breathe, food to eat, and even water to drink - if you know how to make it that is. In fact, the ocean is filled with all the opportunities we need to thrive. Yet for all the resources the sea has available, it doesn't make it easy to get to them. Indeed, there are high waves and strong currents, no shelter from the hot sun or heavy storms, and even the water itself is filled with salt - meaning you can't readily drink it from the source – making it effectively a desert. But if you build a sturdy ship, learn to swim, understand how to fish, know what to look for, how to navigate, and even learned some desalination techniques, you can master the sea, travel the world, and make yourself a success.

Throughout our lives, an ocean of opportunity exists out there, waiting for us to seize it all and take advantage of it to make ourselves successful. Yet most of the time, in order to find and take advantage of those opportunities, you'll have to be able to think creatively and critically about how to get to them and use them. The problem is, that the vast majority of people in our age are only ever taught "what" to think during their lives, as schools and society no longer teach people "how" to think. Most of our education today has become nothing more than indoctrination, teaching the coming generations what to think based on the biased and heavily skewed opinions of those whose positions are deeply rooted in a self-imposed bubble in ignorance.

The reality is, life is filled with an infinite number of unique problems to which no solution has been thought of yet. Though you've never been taught the answer to these problems, if you knew "how" to think around them, you can solve them and find the right solution. But if you never learn "how" to think constructively, creatively, and critically, you won't know what to look for or how to use your skills to get what you need to survive. If you don't know how to think around the problems, you're likely to encounter while crossing the desert, you'll quickly succumb to even the smallest amount of adversity blocking your path... This is because, when you're only ever taught "what" to think, you're placed in a bubble, and if you don't know the answer already when encountering a new and unique problem, you're doomed to failure.

Today is a day to challenge your ability to "think". It is almost guaranteed that you've been slowly indoctrinated throughout your life with horrible biases on what others want you to think and believe. It's very likely your decisions are rote, your solutions are pre-learned, and your judgments are emotionally driven. It's far less likely that anyone taught you "how" to challenge what you think and believe, in order to problem solve, learn, and grow, and how to reason with constructive and critical thought. Far less likely that you were taught to let reality and facts change your mind, your perspective, and your position, and how to engage effectively to creatively solve problems you've never encountered before and have no answer for.

An ocean filled with opportunities may be there waiting for you, but almost always they won't be readily recognizable nor readily accessible. They will nearly always come hidden within adversity, disguised as hardship, and require solutions to seize them that might be outside the box. The key to finding and taking advantage of them is learning how to effectively consider the methods of reaching them... And that's a skill you'll never learn by being indoctrinated into "what" others want you to think.

SOMETHING NEW EVERY DAY

Submarines...

Naval instruments of stealth warfare. Designed purposely with the capability to silently stalk prey and sink enemy ships, today they fulfill a multitude of tactical and strategic roles in both national defense and force projection.

From conventional and nuclear strike capabilities, to special reconnaissance and intelligence, to special warfare support, to scientific research and exploration, and even calls to aid and search and rescue, naval submarines have come a long way from their original singular design purpose. They've evolved and adapted to fit the needs and demands of our age. This is exactly what makes submarines so important to the total force, prized members of the team even to this day...

As time has marched on, new threats have emerged, and the shape of warfare has changed to meet the needs of commanders addressing those threats. Gone are the days where the enemy and the battlefield were clearly defined; today the warzone is asymmetric in nature, and a growing demand for adaptability and diversification in capabilities has become the defining trait of effective teams...

Just like the submarine, we too as individuals must learn to adapt ourselves to ever-changing, dynamic environments. We must seek to continuously evolve if we are ever to remain an asset to our teams. Merely maintaining one or two capabilities is not good enough anymore, we must be capable of bringing a myriad of traits and skills to the table. We must seek never-ending, continuous growth if we are ever going to remain effective, efficient, and relevant to the challenges of today and tomorrow.

Today, take some time to learn this lesson well... Teams are only as strong and capable as their weakest link.

Of all the naval ships out there, submarines have always been at the tip of the spear, not only due to their first-strike capabilities but for their sheer versatility and adaptability as well. Just like the submarine, you too should seek to continuously grow, adapt, and diversify your knowledge, skills, and abilities. Don't allow yourself to become your team's weak link, stay at the forefront, BE the tip of the spear. Learn something new every day. Exercise the mind, body, AND soul, every day. Seek to grow, even if just a little, every, single day, so that you too will bring an array of possibilities and capabilities to your team.

It's not as if growth happens overnight. Instead, focus on improving weak areas over time while developing yourself in new areas to match the demands of the mission at hand. But like the submarine, if you want to stay relevant, you need to grow and adapt to changing environments, mission needs, and team requirements. To Lead from the Front, you have to bring more to the fight each day than you did the day before. Otherwise... Don't expect yourself to remain a prized member of the team.

SPATIAL DISORIENTATION

Amongst the vastness of the open sea, void of reference points in all directions, and enveloped within a dense fog, it isn't difficult for even the sturdiest sailor to become spatially disorientated. We may easily get the feeling we're going in one direction when the truth is, we're going the opposite. We may feel like we're on a relatively stable course, and before we know it, the world is spinning. We could become so fixated on the task at hand, that we forget to look at everything else going on around us. Another objects' movement may make us feel like we're moving, we may confuse the size of an on-coming obstacle blocking our path, or we may end up going in circles without knowing we're going in circles... Spatial disorientation occurs whenever the brain has trouble interpreting the information we're seeing and feeling from the world around us, and it can and will lead us astray... Or worse, it can be deadly.

Just like a pilot in the air, a diver under the waves, or a sailor out at sea, you are not impervious to becoming disorientated along your journey, and if you're not careful, you could become incapacitated and end your quest prematurely. But like the pilot, the diver, and the sailor, you have instruments and tools readily available that can help prevent such incidents from occurring, or that can help you get out of developed disorientation after it has occurred. You simply need to learn how to use them and trust that they will guide you the right way.

To properly prevent yourself from becoming disorientated, you need to continuously cross-check the information you receive, you need to verify that you're on the right path, headed the right direction, maintaining an appropriate speed, and making progress. You need to know what to expect, what's coming your way, what to avoid, and what corrections to make ahead of time. You can do this by double checking your progress against multiple sources of information, getting constructive feedback from outside sources, and even by keeping a daily log to track your progress. Using these tools and instruments appropriately can greatly aid you in staying true to your intended course. These things can help you to understand your situation by giving you reference points... They will allow you to see through the fog and guide you like a compass and sextant to your intended destination.

Today, simply stop and reflect on your progress so far... You've undoubtedly made great strides since your journey began, but have you been cross-checking to assure you're staying on a positive path? Or have you become spatially disorientated, going in circles, redirected without knowing it, fixated on one thing while ignoring all the more important things around you that could have helped you stay on target? Do you have a log from which to track and verify your progress? Have you sought out information from outside sources, from those who can see what you can't see yourself? Even the most experienced aviator needs instruments to tell them where they are, even the most experienced sailor needs many tools and charts to guide them, and even the most experienced diver needs feedback and a cautious attitude to make it back safely.

Stop and consider... Are you still on the right course? If not, now's the time to focus on making the corrections needed to realign yourself with the goal in mind.

TAKE ACTION TODAY

So many people out there have dreams they strive for in their lives. They want to be a part of something amazing, larger than life, bigger than themselves, and they want to accomplish great and meaningful things... YOU are no different.

The problem is that, while people are focused on striving toward their dreams, many miss opportunities that come along the way each and every day. Opportunities to impact lives, to measure up, to leave their mark, to create change, and to make a real difference in the world... Remember yesterday when we talked about Spatial Disorientation? Well, many people become so fixated on their future dreams, that they completely miss tons of small opportunities that can help them get where they want to go. Opportunities that can better themselves and their team, to help them reach the next level, and ultimately achieve success.

While it's highly important for you to keep a long-term goal in mind, you shouldn't let that goal become your singular focus. There's so much more, happening right now this very second, that needs your attention, and if you fail to notice it all, you very well could lose someone or something important to you. You could lose family and friends, valued team members, trust and respect from peers, and even miss impending dangers headed your way. Complacency kills, and we become complacent to the world around us when we get too comfortable with the daily grind. This eventually causes us to ignore things our brain thinks aren't necessary to pay attention to... Which is exactly what happens when we become Fascinated or Fixated on that far-off goal.

Work toward your dreams, absolutely! Your dreams are important... But don't lose focus of the here and now. Don't let your efforts of striving toward your future dreams prevent you from taking real actions today, from paying attention to the world around you today, from being here – present – for those who need you TODAY. After all, it's what you're capable of doing, what you're able to do, what you actually do, right now, today, that matters most... And so long as your actions are positive, just, honorable, and of service to others, I will tell you... That you ARE creating an impact, changing lives, and making a REAL difference in the world.

TODAY, take some time to consider if you've become fixated on those dreams you see resting up high on that mountain in the distance. Consider if you've missed some opportunities to make a real difference in the here-and-now... A difference in the lives of those around you, for a complete stranger, and even for yourself. Often times, when we pursue a personal goal and take to an endeavor meaningful to us, we have a strong tendency to think about and look only at that goal in mind, and as we do, we completely miss all the life that is happening around us. Like driving fast down the street in a car, the scenery becomes a passing blur while we focus on making that next turn to reach our destination on time... It's times like that, we miss important opportunities that add up to success.

If the scenery of your life has become a passing blur, you've more than likely become fixated on your future goals and are missing daily opportunities along the way. Perhaps consider walking next time? You just might notice opportunities you never knew about when you were fixated on simply getting there the day before.

LOOK FORWARD TO THE SUNRISE

I know I've said this countless times before in my life... I am NOT a "Morning Person"... But I HAVE grown to appreciate the beauty of a sunrise.

Have you ever watched a sunrise?

Have you ever sat patiently, in silence, and watched in admiration as the sun peaked up slowly over the horizon and greeted you on a brand-new day? Have you ever marveled in awe at the sheer magnitude of the event as it unfolds before your eyes, and felt the blessings of its warm rays filling the world with life? Let me tell you... Being greeted by the sun first thing in the morning is highly motivational for me. It represents the dawn of a new day, new beginnings, a fresh start, a chance for change. And most of all... The blessing of even having another day to walk this earth coming along with it.

Think about it... We're not guaranteed tomorrow, and our time in life is short and fleeting. We miss out on so very much each day as we get wrapped up in work, in tasks, in excuses... In what the world tells us and tries to convince us is "important" (but really isn't) ... At times, life seems to move at a million miles an hour, and with it, our time is lost. We forget "time" is our most precious and valuable resource, and we only have just so much of it. Once it's gone, it's gone, and that's that...

Yet the sun rising at the dawn of a new day brings with it all new opportunities for a fresh start, a chance to lead off with a strong step, and the possibilities of accomplishing something you couldn't the day before. It brings with it new beginnings from which we might grasp hold of, cherish, and be ever thankful for. To this day, I'm STILL not a "morning person" ... But I thoroughly appreciate the beauty and marvel of a sunrise and am thankful for all the new possibilities that come along with it.

So today, I challenge you to do the same...

If you're an "I'm not a Morning Person" type of person, like me, perhaps you too can learn to find motivation in the thought of being greeted by the rising sun. It's a spectacular sight, to say the least! It's a thing of beauty MOST of us take for granted, and some of us have never once truly admired... And if the idea of a fresh start greeted by the rising sun isn't motivating enough for you to appreciate the start of a brand-new day with... At the very least, you can admire the sheer beauty the sun brings with it and let that start your day off with some positivity in mind.

After all, the day will ultimately be what you chose to make of it... So why not make it a positive one? We tend to do our best work when high on a positive note... So even here you have an opportunity for self-betterment in simply starting the day by seeing the sunrise as something motivating... And that's worth admiring, isn't it?

FAIR SEAS NEVER MADE A SKILLFUL SAILOR

There exist two types of sailors in life, and as you've now been out to sea for a while, fast approaching the land you've been aiming for, you've undoubtedly met one of the two far more frequently than the other along the way.

There's the Captain and the Yachtsman.

The Captain is a master of his destiny, his craft, his profession, and of himself. He seeks to develop his skills and broaden his knowledge in all aspects of his chosen way of life and puts that knowledge and those skills frequently to the test in application. He actively uses what life throws his way to grow, finds opportunity in adversity, and never shies away from a challenge. Competent and confident, his mission and his crew come first, and training, planning, and preparation assure his success. Circumstances don't define his life, his choices do, and his character is a testament to the acceptance of personal responsibility and accountability.

The Yachtsman, on the other hand, is looking for a pleasure cruise... He is no true sailor, no adventurer, no warrior, and no leader... No. He's a weekend hobbyist playing the part while looking to benefit from the hard work and sacrifice of others. The first to pull into port at the sight of bad weather and the one who stays home when the seas are rough. A regular hang around at the local watering hole, while the Captain is braving the storm to accomplish the mission, the Yachtsman is telling fish stories to the ignorant who admire and believe him. He's the unprepared and unskilled, who without a shred of bravery, cowers when caught in the clutches of adversity, then suggests he's a victim of circumstance. Nothing is ever truly his fault, and cursing every hardship, he never grows.

The seas are filled with Yachtsmen pretending to be Captains, and they're not hard to spot. A little discomfort is often all it takes to reveal the true nature of an unskilled coward who blames the world for all their woes. They'll quickly take credit for tall tales and success stories, yet are somehow never responsible for mistakes. These are individuals who are unteachable. They're brick walls who refuse to listen, who always believe they are right, they know everything, and no amount of facts or experience will ever convince them otherwise. These are people who will never grow, and they will never reach that mountain in the distance because of it.

Today's a day to learn from bad examples – and this is the only time I'll suggest you ever try to learn a lesson from bad examples. Don't be a Yachtsman. Remember... Adversity is one of life's greatest teachers. If you'd only just listen, you'd hear some of the wisest words in existence... That every hardship is a lesson, and every setback is an opportunity for growth. Challenge is your friend, and personal responsibility and accountability the foundations of good character. Life is filled to the hilt with storms that bring strong winds and high waves, and if you never seek out challenge, you'll never rise to the occasion when needed most. If you never seek growth, you'll never reach your dreams. I'd rather have a skillful sailor – a Captain whose skills have been trained, refined and proven in rough seas - on my team any day, than a Yachtsman who refuses to sail without calm seas and cowers in the face of a little wind.

THE CAPTAIN OF YOUR SOUL

Out of the night that covers me,
　　Black as the pit from pole to pole,
I thank whatever gods may be
　　For my unconquerable soul.

In the fell clutch of circumstance
　　I have not winced nor cried aloud.
Under the bludgeonings of chance
　　My head is bloody but unbowed.

Beyond this place of wrath and tears
　　Looms but the Horror of the shade,
And yet the menace of the years
　　Finds, and shall find me, unafraid.

It matters not how strait the gate,
　　How charged with punishments the scroll,
I am the master of my fate:
　　I am the captain of my soul.

Invictus – William Ernest Henley (1888)

Dry land at last. You've stepped foot on the beach. The days of trial on the open seas are now behind you, but the lessons you've learned will become the tools required to meet the challenges ahead of you. Stopping to look back, you remember how difficult it was to leave the comfortable land you came from, and sail an expanse of ocean to reach the land you stand on now. As you reflect on how far you've come, the thought should be present in your mind...

YOU made that choice... Not fate, not peers, not society... You did, and no matter how hard or difficult that choice was, no matter what pain and hardship that came along with it, you were able to overcome them all simply by refusing to give up, give in, and quit. You chose to take command of your life, to become the master of your fate, and take the reigns as captain of your soul. No matter what crossed your path, what storms raged, or waves crashed down upon you, you faced them head-on, learned from them, grew stronger because of them, and smiled on the other side.

Latin for "unconquerable" or "undefeated", "Invictus" highlights the lesson you should have learned by now... That the idea of ever being conquered or defeated in your life is entirely up to you. That the only one and the only thing that can ever seal your fate and guarantee your defeat in life is you. Today marks the solidification of that foundation to your growth... Not wrath nor circumstance, nor the bludgeonings of chance can make you bow. No... Your life is your own making, and you've accepted that as fact. So, say it with me...

"I am the master of my fate; I am the captain of my soul."

Powerful words for which to live your life by... You CHOOSE to either be a slave to the circumstances of your life, or you decide for yourself to take command of your life. Today marks the start of the next phase of your journey. You're now equipped with the foundation and resolve required to move on to greater heights. You can accomplish anything, meet any challenge, rise to any occasion, so long as you believe you can.

The poem Invictus is a powerful reminder that we can overcome any and all odds, that ownership and acceptance of personal accountability and responsibility speaks volumes about your character, that we're stronger and more capable than the world would like to have us believe, and that what matters MOST in life is not whether or not you've survived life's storms, it's how you chose to face adversity, trial, hardship, and challenges when they came.

The next great challenge is before you... Are you ready?

You should be.

THE MOUNTAIN WITH NO SUMMIT

Every journey has points at which you can validate meaningful accomplishment. Times when you can look back and reflect to see you've made progress. Where you can recall events that tested your soul, where you had to make some tough decisions, and the result of those decisions either crippled you, bruised you, or saved you, but all stood equal opportunity to grow you... And here you are, still standing tall. You weathered great trials on high waves, endured life's storms and basked in the warmth of the sun... You crossed a great sea and made it to the land of that mountain where success can be found... THIS is one of those moments! THIS is one of those points at which you can look back and see that you have accomplished something great and meaningful and overcame seemingly impossible odds that made you better along the way!

But now, standing on the shoreline, you turn to face forward, to begin the next great phase of your quest... And upon looking at the path before your feet, reality begins to set in... Standing at the entrance to the valley that rests at the foot of that mountain, and lifting up your eyes, you come face-to-face with the truth... The path you committed yourself to long ago, hasn't gotten any easier... In fact, it seems to have only gotten more difficult at best... The path you find before you now, you realize, is going to be perilous, arduous work... That's just the cold, hard fact of life.

Turning your gaze skyward reveals an imposing view... A mountain of unfathomable height, filled with perils, adversity, trials, and hardships, and no summit to be found... There's no set path, no transportation, no easy routes, and no short cuts... Yet somewhere up high, just beyond sight, beyond the clouds and near the stars, your hopes and dreams can be found waiting for you to reach them and achieve them. You've come so far already, you're so close, yet still so far away... The only method possible of reaching those dreams is for you to simply climb the mountain.

It's an awe-inspiring and yet impossibly absurd notion... That the journey to our individual development and success is like climbing a mountain with no summit... And yet, the comparison of personal development to the idea of a journey with no end in sight is not only appropriate, but it's also inspiringly accurate! Stretching skyward with no end in sight, it means no matter how far you've gone, you'll always have more to go, no matter how fast you climb, you'll never reach the top... But that's the beauty of it! It means, so long as you're willing to make progress, you'll always have room to grow and there'll always be something you can improve upon! Leadership development IS personal development, and personal development is an individually motivated, never-ending process!

It's a journey that few embark upon, and it's exactly the reason why there are so few TRUE "leaders" in the world...

Taking a second to look around, you'll quickly find many others standing in the midst of that valley, staring upward at the mountain, and yet... That's exactly all the vast majority of them are doing... Standing and staring, and nothing more. You'll notice most of them turn their back on the mountain, and uttering every excuse imaginable for why it's "impossible", they'll retreat back into their tents – those made of shallowness, weakness, ignorance, and bias – refusing to leave the valley because they refuse to do the hard work and make the sacrifices required to survive the climb. They've set up camp here and quit their journey. But there's a difference between them and you... Whereas the majority are unwilling to climb for any number of excuses, you're ready and willing to get going.

Today, consider carefully your own Mountain with No Summit and think whether or not you're ready and willing to begin the eternal climb. It starts with a step, and then another, and another, and you're off. Braving the perils and enduring the hardships, you'll grow strong, wise, and resilient as your character is molded and shaped by each day's climb. Before long, you'll be able to look back and behold an amazing sight... Marveling at how far you've gone, you'll discover a long line of others also starting to climb right behind you, walking in your footsteps, and using the path you've paved as their guide for forward progress. You'll discover the true side effect of working hard toward self-betterment... You'll discover you've become a true leader... You'll lead intrinsically... You'll lead from the front... You'll become a leader by example.

The mountain stands before us all... You've come THIS far... Choose not to live in the valley.

THE START OF EACH DAY

Your journey to success starts each day long before the sun rises, before the rest of the world opens their eyes, before the sound of the first alarm goes off, before the first sip of coffee, before the morning shave, and indeed before the first foot hits the floor... It begins in the early morning hours with you, a decision, and some motivation. Before the rest of the world cracks open their eyes, you've already dressed, laced up, grabbed your pack, and stepped off. By the time the rest of the world seeks to begin their day, they'll look out upon the horizon, blinded by morning rays, and what will they find?

You...

The silhouette of success in the making, basked in the sunlight's warm morning glow as if born from the very rays themselves, having already been at it for hours... Leading the way to glory.

The journey to success started long before you were ever ready to take the journey in the first place. In fact, it started with your decision to commit to taking the journey. Through your time so far, you've grown stronger and wiser and prepared yourself for greater challenges yet to come. But if you're ever going to get ahead, the REAL effort will take place in the hours while the rest of the world is still only dreaming of success, and that means you'll make the most progress in those early-morning hours as well.

During any long-distance journey, it's important to maximize the time you are blessed with each day. Waking up and getting in some miles before the sun rises takes serious commitment to stick with, but that developed habit is what sets you apart from the mediocre who chose to sleep in every day. While the rest of the world is dreaming of getting into shape, striking business deals, making progress on their book, pursuing education, and reaching the stars, you've already finished your run, shook hands with a new partner, written another chapter, studied for that next exam, and started your climb to the top.

Today, consider this... Early to rise; early to success. Today, start working on developing a habit of being early to rise – if you haven't already. While the world is still asleep, you'll get a head start. While your competition is still dreaming of achievement, you'll have already made progress toward it. While the rest of the world is still fat and lazy, complaining about not having time to get into shape, you'll be in shape, and know where that time is found. While the enemy sleeps, you'll be arriving on the 'X". And while your team is still resting, as a leader, you can help set them – and yourself – up for success. Being successful in life requires we sacrifice some things to get there. Most people dream of success yet complain that they can't "find" the time to make it happen. But the truth is, like my father once told me as a child... If something is important to you, you MAKE the time.

The path is already at your feet, the mountain sits before you, and the clock is ticking... Are you still merely dreaming of the goal? Or have you been at it for hours now, before everyone else woke up, making steady progress while the rest of the world merely dreams of success?

ENCOUNTERING "UNKNOWNS"

What lies just beyond the bend? Well... You don't know, but should that stop you from finding out? Nothing ventured, nothing gained, and if you refuse to move forward despite the "unknowns" awaiting before you, you'll never discover what possibilities might be within your reach, now will you?

Your life is a path filled with unknown possibilities lurking just beyond its many twists and turns, and your growth is the act of you walking forward despite what you might encounter along the way. The good, the bad, the ugly, and even the simply amazing, will cross your path. Sometimes you'll have the opportunity of seeing them in advance, and many times, you won't... But making the conscious choice to move forward, regardless, is what enables you to grow. And striving through the bad and the ugly with courage, while humbly accepting the good when it comes your way, is what defines an indomitable spirit of strength, and a character worthy of respect.

And THAT makes YOU inspiring to others...

Your journey to climb the mountain SHOULD rightfully be one filled with new experiences. You should be seeking out new information, new opportunities, and new challenges every day. Things you've never seen before, heard before, felt before, or encountered before. If you're going to grow and make progress, you'll need to be willing to actively seek out encounters with the unknown, to be willing to move forward despite the possibility of coming face-to-face with bad experiences and failures.

If you ever find you're not encountering any new "unknowns" in your life, there's a strong possibility you've stopped walking your path. If you find you're not making new discoveries and the adventure no longer feels like "an adventure", you've more than likely plateaued and started playing it safe. You've stopped progressing, stopped moving forward, and started stagnating. You set up camp and started living in a bubble, and if that's the case, you might as well just be dead. For when we stop growing, we start dying...

You've been at it for a while now... So, today's a day to ponder if the adventure – your adventure – still feels like one. Are you still moving forward? Or has the idea of your journey become merely a routine? If so, then you need to start looking for a new path that keeps you interested, keeps it fresh, and keeps you learning, progressing, and experiencing new things! Keep moving forward! Look forward to encountering whatever you will find just beyond the next bend and be thankful for it. If it's something good, great! But if it's something bad, just remember... It's actually a blessing meant to prepare you for operating at higher levels later in life.

The last thing you want to allow to happen is using the idea of not knowing what might happen as an excuse to keep you where you're at right now. Once that happens, you stop carving a path and start setting up camp... And setting up camp where you're at now is NOT what this journey is about... right?

THE MANY CURVES OF LIFE

Your journey through life is bound to have many twists and turns, and very often you won't know what lies just around the bend. Obstacles like large rocks and hills, forests and changing terrain will obstruct our view, and there won't always be signs available to warn you of what is coming up around the next corner. The truth of the matter is, there will inevitably be many times when you simply won't know what will happen next, and upon approaching a curve in your path, you're left with a choice as to how to proceed.

The foolhardy would fly through the curves at speed, daringly with unchecked confidence. The wise, on the other hand, would exercise caution with the unknown while proceeding onwards. Everything may seem fine and the path may appear easy if the road ahead is straight, but the truth is, there never really is a completely straight path to reach our destination. Sure, you may see where you want to go off in the distance, but to get there will require you to traverse difficult terrain and carve a new path along the way. Just like the storms encountered during your sea-faring days, the road ahead is filled with challenges yet to come. And just like how you chose to face those storms when they came, it's how you choose to handle the curves ahead that will define your character.

The choices we make when curves come up can either benefit us, or crash us head-on into unforeseen obstacles, and that's the point. You never really know what you'll encounter as you move forward. Making serious progress undoubtedly requires a bit of tenacity, sure, but only a fool would throw caution to the wind and sprint forward blindly. Making wise choices would,

therefore, seem the right thing to always do, yet I ask you...
...Are you really living if you never take a chance or two?

Consider carefully how you choose to answer that, after all, it may not be only you, but your team as well, that could benefit or suffer the consequences...

Today, stop and think about the actions you take when encountering a sudden curve in your path. Having a plan for your future progression is great, but as Murphy once said, no good plan ever survives first contact. Do you know how you'll take the next corner? Will you alter your gait as you approach so your outside foot hits just beyond the corner, allowing you to execute a quick turn and put eyes on any unknown threats? Will you pause briefly at the corner to get a quick glance prior to making the turn, allowing you to judge if anything is there or not before proceeding? Will you utilize tools to help you peer just beyond the bend? Do you have a variety of alternative courses of action or contingencies if you did encounter a problem or threat?

You have a mission to accomplish, and you already know full well you're going to proceed and move forward toward reaching the goal... But how will you handle the curves you must take to make progress toward reaching that goal? Just remember, there's no clearly defined path, and as such, no one correct answer either.

MAKE YOUR OWN PATH

Walking a path through the forest isn't always as easy as it sounds. Embarking on a trek to reach an intended destination will quickly become an exercise in dealing with the wilderness itself more so than simply navigating your way through it. Tall trees will prevent you from seeing what's off in the distance. Thick vines will become nets impeding progress. Bushes and underbrush can hide sharp branches, thorns, and natural traps. And everything from rocky cliffs and sharp changes in terrain, to rivers with no banks, will force you to change directions in order to keep going... It sounds easier than it really is... "Walk through the forest, and into the valley, to reach that mountain off in the distance..." But when we actually take to doing it, we quickly discover no true path exists, and we have a choice to make...

Do we give up? Do we keep looking for a path already made? Or do we strike out to make our own path?

After spending weeks at sea, and finally arriving on the other side, it's easy to fall into the trap of believing you've left the ocean behind you. So much of the time while dreaming of our future success we fail to notice we encountered a NEW "sea" and we didn't even realize it... We encountered a Sea of Forest impeding our way, blocking our path, impeding our vision, and leading us in circles. It's easy to get lost in a sea of trees, so most people seek the easy way out... They try their hardest to find a path someone else has already carved. And when they don't find one, most give up. Resigning themselves to being lost, they quit.

Look, no one said it would ever be easy, but the goal is just on the other side! What's stopping you from reaching it? A little problem-solving and hard work?

Think about it! You navigated across one ocean already, haven't you? That means you already KNOW "how" to navigate, right? You encountered obstacles and blockades, hidden dangers and unexpected problems along the way... So, you know how to plan, mitigate, and adapt to overcome... How is this "sea" any different? It only LOOKS different, but you have all the skills and tools necessary readily at your disposal, all you have to do is adapt them to fit this new situation to be successful!

And THAT's what today is all about!

Consider this... Throughout your life, you'll likely encounter many "seas"; problems and situations you'll have to navigate through in order to achieve success. They'll come in all different shapes and sizes, and they'll often look like completely different and new experiences you never encountered before... But that's wrong. If you look closely enough, you'll discover many commonalities shared between them, and with that, find you already have the knowledge, skills, and abilities (KSA's) required to make it through... You have all the tools you need to move forward; all YOU have to do is be willing to make your own path!

There is no one set path to reaching our dreams, and eventually, you'll have to make your own path through life's forests. But I guarantee you this... When you look back from the other side, you'll realize how easy it was, how much stronger you became as a result, and when you achieve your goals, you'll admit it was worth it. Sometimes there will be a clear path in front of you, and sometimes you'll have to make one yourself. The only real question you have to ask yourself is...

Are you willing?

YOU CAN'T CHEAT YOUR WAY TO SUCCESS

2nd Timothy, 2:5 (KJV) - "And if a man also strives for masteries, yet is he not crowned, except he strives lawfully."

In other words, you can't win the prize unless you play by the rules. You can't cheat your way to success anymore than you can shortcut your way to master an art or skill.

We ALL start our journey standing at the shore of a perilous sea. Somewhere beyond the other side exists a valley, at the foot of which stands a mountain with no summit. Our goals, hopes, and dreams rest somewhere up high on that mountain and yet stretched out before us life bears no readily made path to reach them...

Gazing outward upon the journey at our feet we find only hardship, trials, adversity, and many great unknowns. The sea is fraught with storms and high waves, the valley is thick with forests and predators, and the mountain... Tall, steep, cold with high winds, and endless in height... Should you try to embark to seek your goals, you could be crushed and sunk to the depths, lost in the wilderness, eaten by predators, frozen by wind and snow, or even lose your grip and fall... To think, even for a second, that you can simply demand your way to the end, or wish your way to the top, that you're somehow, for some reason, "entitled" to the reward without taking the journey for yourself, would be ignorant at best.

To earn your reward, you'll have to carve your own path, brave the seas, face the storms, grit your teeth, and endure... And even after you make it across the seas, tread over desert expanses, and navigate through the forests… You'll discover the REAL journey finally begins as you take to climbing that mountain. No… There are no shortcuts to success… Success MUST be earned. And if you strive for a mastery of any kind, you have absolutely no choice but to take the journey to EARN the crown.

Today is a day to think carefully about all the times you've attempted to cheat your way to success. How many times have you cut corners? How many times have you cut in line? How many times have you attempted to shortcut your way to the goal? How many times have you granted yourself a little extra when no one was looking? How many times have you attempted to bend the rules, or worse… Arrogantly and hypocritically pretended the rules that apply to all equally didn't apply to yourself? How many times have you tried to justify it all to yourself by telling yourself it doesn't really matter either?

The rules of the universe are simple… If you want the reward, you have to put in the effort. You're NOT "special", you're NOT some kind of "exception", and a false belief that you're "entitled" won't magically transport you to the top. Cheating won't get you there any faster, and if anything, could set you back, you could get seriously hurt, or worse, it could end your journey completely. Today… Spend the day reflecting on all the times you tried to cheat… Then focus on committing here and now to honest hard work in the future to reach your dreams.

YOUR BUBBLE OF COMFORT

The vast majority of people out there will never achieve their goals, will never overcome their problems, and they will never see true progress in their lives. While you're out starting your climb, traveling the world, seeing and experiencing new things, breaking barriers, overcoming odds, and growing... The vast majority of people peaked in high school. Years later, they're still rotting away in the same old town, complaining about the same old things, living with the same old problems, and experiencing the same old hardships... Why? Because they're filled with the disease of mediocrity and in love with their comfort zone. THAT's why.

Understand this... It takes an extraordinarily strong internally motivated desire to break free of your comfortable bubble – filled with ignorance, biases, mediocrity, and more – to overcome your excuses, break barriers, and achieve greatness in life. REAL success comes from learning to become comfortable with "being uncomfortable", and this is something – at THIS point – that you should be readily familiar with.

There exists a bubble for our lives, containing all our securities, all the things that make us feel comfortable in life, and its gravitational pull is severely strong. Outside of it is a void, an expanse, beyond which rests a zone of discomfort where our dreams become possible. The gravity pulling us in is our desire to remain comfortable, and the barriers preventing us from leaving are made from our excuses. Like a prisoner, you're trapped and held captive, yet your desire to succeed can overcome that gravitational pull (if only you'd nurture it), and your internalized motivation to achieve can become the bridge that spans the void and leads you beyond your comfort zone, to a place where real change can happen, where real education occurs, where real growth takes place, and where success is made possible.

Today is a day to search for and discover any last remaining "bubbles of comfort" that may be holding you back. Now's the time, before the REAL journey starts to get serious, to rid yourself of the dead weight holding you back. Your desire to remain comfortable, no matter how small or subtle, will prevent you from making the climb that stands before you.

Real growth isn't possible without the discomfort of hard work, real success isn't possible without the discomfort of overcoming obstacles, and real character isn't possible without the discomfort of overcoming adversity. Your dreams are not possible to reach without weathering the discomfort of the journey required to reach them. So if you ever want to grow, ever want to learn, ever want to achieve, and ever want to succeed, cast off your bubble, abandon your comfort, and Embrace the Suck! Learn to become comfortable with the idea of living your life in a constant state of discomfort, because it is there that these things are made possible.

You can do it, ANYONE can do it, you just have to want it bad enough, and that's one of the many reasons so few ever do... So don't tell me you can or you will... SHOW me.

EMBRACE "THE SUCK"

From personal failures to disappointments, from people letting you down to failing because of someone else's lack of responsibility, and from being forced to repeat the same actions over again to working extra hard due to being short-handed, the situations you'll likely encounter may end up being bad, they may be miserable, and they may out-right just suck... But no matter what, the mission doesn't stop. Life doesn't stop just because you're forced to deal with miserable situations. No... You still have a job to do, a mission to accomplish, a goal to reach, and that means there will be times when you simply have to pick up your pack and drive on despite the miserable situation you're currently in... We call that, "The Suck".

It's the conscious acceptance or appreciation of something that is extremely unpleasant but unavoidable for forward progression...

Embrace "The Suck!"

Deal with it! Accept it as an unavoidable fact of life. Welcome it with open arms and learn to live with it. You have no choice but to deal with it, but if you refuse to succumb to it, you can very well push through it. Understand that no matter what, there will be miserable situations you'll be forced to deal with that are unavoidable. You won't be able to escape them, but if you simply reconcile to yourself that they will happen, that there's no changing that fact, and no, there's absolutely NOTHING you can do about it, you'll learn to embrace them as a simple fact of life, and move on... And THAT is how you ultimately set yourself free from them.

There's no rest for those on the road to achievement, the journey to success, the path to greatness... When you made up your mind to embark, gathered your resolve, and took the first steps, you made a commitment to cast aside your worthless, lazy bubble of comfort, weakness, ignorance, and bias. Yet in doing so, you're also willingly admitting that you KNOW you're bound to encounter hardship and adversity along the way. You'll be bombarded by pettiness and evils, encounter violence and suffer loss, and be forced to deal with daily pains and soreness...

THAT'S LIFE! Deal with it!

Today's a day to reconcile every menial chore, every worthless task, and every stupidly painful experience you're forced to deal with just to get through the day... They may suck, but those things are TEMPORARY. You're on the path to greatness! You still have a journey you're committed to and a mission to accomplish! You have no choice but to deal with them, but the journey doesn't stop just because of them either! Embrace the Suck! Learn to accept hardship and adversity, for they will teach you, guide you, and strengthen you. Face every challenge with some backbone and a smile, and every obstacle in your path with honor and a bit of tenacity! And when you feel the urge to "rest" and hear the call of "comfort" beckoning to you from the distance... Remind yourself why you stepped off on your journey in the first place! Then tell those evil whispers that "rest" shall be the reward you'll receive after a life lived to the fullest, and comfort shall come in the arms of the Lord!

— Day 49 —

TAKE EVERY OPPORTUNITY

If you're ever going to reach that next precipice, if you're ever going to make that next ledge, if you're ever going to scale that rock face before you, you'll need to take hold of every advantage you come across, every bit of leverage, and make use of every tool in your inventory. You're on your climb, you've left the ground, and you're making progress, but with progress comes altitude. The increasing distance between yourself and the ground far below will make anyone realize the position they're in and appreciate whatever opportunities to safely proceed they encounter along the way. If you want to successfully make the climb, then heed these words...

Take advantage of every opportunity that comes your way. Grasp it firmly with both hands, use it to your advantage, capitalize on it to grow, and be thankful that the Lord provided it for you in the first place...

Life is short, and time is both limited and fleeting. In a universe where all resources are finite, time is the most precious resource we have, so use it wisely... Only so many opportunities will cross our paths in that time, so seize hold of every one you can. Most of those opportunities will be hidden behind the mask of hardship, so learn to see through the masks. With a limited amount of time and a limited number of opportunities, learn to cherish every moment, because before you know it, that time will be gone.

Enjoy every second life gives to you, and every experience, both the good and the bad, for both teach us valuable lessons, grant us cherished memories, and help us grow. Stray not purposely from adversity, but that doesn't mean you should invite it upon you. If given the choice, choose a positive path and a positive attitude. Yet if adversity and hardship should block your path, stand tall and face them with courage. Find the hidden opportunities they bring with them and use them as tools to your advantage and be thankful and humble when you reach the other side.

Give life EVERYTHING you got, every day, and with purpose and a positive, can-do attitude, sprint toward your goals till you have nothing left... Then keep going! Because THAT is how you make progress! THAT is how you climb the mountain.

Today, take some time to reevaluate how you use your time. Do you use it wisely? Do you capitalize on opportunities? Do you seek to find the hidden ones lurking within a bad situation? Do you face hardships head-on with a positive attitude though they may suck? Are you thankful? Consider this... Very often people forget that life is fragile and short. They mistakenly believe they have "All the time in the world" and put off opportunities today only to discover they became missed opportunities from yesterday. It isn't until we leave the ground and begin to look down that we realize how valuable our time is and how wisely we should consider spending it...

So, do you give life everything you got? Every day? Today, take some time to give thanks to the Lord for every day you're alive and then contemplate how you can make the most of each day. Because before we know it, our time will be nearing an end, and if we spent our time wisely, we're sure to rest comfortably with no regrets high atop the world, with a feeling of accomplishment, wise and satisfied, filled with love and joy, and confident in where we're headed next.

REFLECTION

A great aid in our journey down the path to self-betterment rests in the honest and purposeful reflection of our past experiences in life. Yet the problem is that people have a strong tendency to allow their past to become a burden that weighs them down. We should never dwell on the past, for a refusal to let go of that which we cannot change is a stumbling block that stagnates our progress... But we should be mindful of our past so we may learn from it, let it guide us, strengthen us, grow us, and help us move forward.

A great many people, far too many to count, carry their past around like bricks in a sack on their back. Past mistakes, feelings of regret, sorrow for those lost, and anger – which can turn into bitterness, hate, and malice – all become needless burdens that weigh us down. People often become fixated on the idea that maybe they could have done something different, maybe they could have tried taking a different path or made a better decision, or if they had simply been present things would have turned out differently... But none of these things are true. When people burden themselves by dwelling on the past, they fail to realize the real truth of the matter... That you can't change the past and dwelling on it accomplishes nothing...

...Nothing except wasting the precious time you have today.

Mistakes will be made in your life. That's a fact. But what's important is to learn from them so you can use that knowledge to become better in the future. Bad things will happen in life. That's a fact. The universe is something beyond our control, and the sooner we come to terms with that, the sooner we can learn to let go of things we can't change. Sorrow and regret are toxic to your health (mentally, physically, and spiritually), and bitterness, hate, and malice will destroy you from the inside out. Carrying around these things will ruin your ability to continue on with your journey, and the last thing you want to see happen is for your own journey to stop short due to self-inflicted wounds.

There's nothing wrong with remembering, but the key is not to dwell. Reflect on what has happened so you can learn from those experiences and cherish both the good and the bad so you can accept them. Accepting your past equals accepting yourself as you are today and learning from it is what allows you to grow and achieve.

Today, take some time to honestly reflect on your life's journey. Do you harbor past regrets? Are the pains of bitterness and anger anchoring you to a past event? Are there experiences you constantly wish you could change? The only way you're ever going to lighten your load is to accept these things as they happened. Learn from them, then let them go, least that which you may regret become a needless burden upon your shoulders. After all, why would you want to climb a mountain while needlessly carrying extra weight?

All of your life experiences have made you who you are today, and accepting your past means accepting yourself for who you are. Accepting yourself is the key to releasing you from that bag of bricks, unlocking your potential and allowing you to move forward. You'll never climb your mountain if you're weighed down, so ask yourself... Just who are you carrying around all those bricks for anyway? Let them go, so you can begin to make real progress.

STANDING YOUR GROUND

Yea, though I walk through the valley of the shadow of death, I will fear no evil. For I own the valley, and the shadow is mine. Therefore, my flock may be at home, and they shall boldly thrive. My valley shall become their safe harbor, and all evils who enter therein to threaten them shall know my wrath. For I am the Arranger of Meetings between my enemies and God, charged to defend the good from the vile evils of the world. Out of love for my flock I Faithfully execute the duties of my position, that no evil shall threaten my house. To this end I shall gladly sacrifice, So Others May Live. The LORD is my strength and my shield, and my heart shall trust in Him. For if God is with me, no evil can be against me, and my home, my valley, shall persevere.

—AJ Powell's Combat Prayer

Society is filled to the ever-livin' HILT with corruption and vileness, and it takes great courage to stand your ground against all the evils of the world. Yet that is your charge as the leader of the pack, to stand up in the face of any who threaten your team. Like a sniper perched on high ground, you look over your team like you look over the valley below. Able to effectively monitor the only entry and exit points, you keep watch for approaching threats and predators that dare to enter and engage when targets cross your path. As you lead your team up the mountain toward the objective, you stand as the defense between your team's success, their ability to thrive and grow, and the sinful world that seeks to lead them astray.

There will be times when you will come face-to-face with the countless great evils of the world. Like David standing up to

Goliath, you may be outclassed, outnumbered, and outgunned. But fear not, for it is in our greatest hours of need, when the enemy may seem overwhelming and we face perilous odds, that you need to remember above all else... You OWN the valley, and the shadow is YOURS. The welfare of YOUR team and the accomplishment of YOUR mission take precedence above yourself, and with the Lord by your side, there exists NO evil that can stand against you. You have the high ground! And with that, you can prevail.

Today's a day to consider what it means to stand your ground. Consider carefully the charge placed upon you as a leader. The welfare of your team and its success are your priorities. If they succeed, you succeed. If they fall to the temptations of the evils of the world, you all fall off the mountain. Make no mistake, you're a wolf, not a sheepdog. Engaging threats BEFORE they can inflict damage is what it takes to protect the team. You should never be a guest in someone else's valley. If you were, then you'd be putting yourself and your team at risk, fearfully walking in the shadow of death. To successfully protect your team, OWN your valley, and become the shadow that evil fears. After all, your job is not to be protected, but to protect. Your job is not to defend, but to hunt. So, own your valley, and let your shadow stretch out before it all, that it might strike fear into any evils that dare, and keep them at bay. And if all else fails you, keep Faith in God, that He will see you through. After all, if God is with you, no evil can be against you. The LORD is your strength and your shield; your heart should trust in Him...

PUSH PAST YOUR LIMITS

So... Let's say you start your days with a morning run. You normally run for an hour, and typically get in seven miles in one hour. This has become your benchmark, your standard. But today isn't about distance. Instead, today you have a goal in mind to run for a certain amount of time. You start your distance tracker, check your watch for the time, make a mental note, and step off.

You've completed this run daily for a while now, so you have a good feel for about how far you can normally go in a given period of time if you maintain a certain pace. You've settled into a nice routine, so this is nothing new. But today, you're not going for "speed" or "distance"... The goal is simply to run for a solid hour, non-stop, no breaks... Just run. You're going for "time", and as you start, you increase your pace by feel until you've reached a comfortable stride... A stride you think would get you the distance you normally track for an hour-long run.

Later, you check your watch and notice you've been running for close to an hour now... The time you're going for is nearly up, and with only a few minutes remaining, you quickly glance at your distance tracker, but to your surprise, what do you see? You find that you're behind your normal time and have missed your normal mark! You're at the end of your hour, but you've only gone six and a half miles!

What do you do?!

Well... MOST people would simply stick to the plan and quit at that hour when they planned to stop running in the first place... But you're NOT "most people". Are you? No... You have established a standard for yourself that you hold yourself accountable to maintain. You need to get in that last half mile! So, you punch it and sprint the last half mile during your typical cool-down period! Your "cool-down" is normally about five minutes, yet only two minutes into it, you hit that seventh mile. You still have three minutes left... What do you do?!!!

That's right! It's ONLY three more minutes!!! YOU SPRINT THAT TOO!

Give it hell! Go as far over the goal as you can with whatever extra time and energy you have left! You OBVIOUSLY took it easy the whole time if you can still sprint full speed now after a full hour, how DARE you! You NEED to get that back! You NEED to make up for it by going the extra distance! Hit it with everything you got and put some emphasis on it! THAT'S what you do! And THAT is how we should live life!

Today, ask yourself if you routinely "go the extra mile". Do you? Or are you the type of person who sticks only to the plan and does the "bare minimum" if that's just how the plan works out? If you're the kind of person who DOESN'T sprint that last half-mile – and THEN some – despite reaching the time limit, next ask yourself, why are you even taking this journey in the first place then?!

Let me tell you something you SHOULD already know... "Moderation" is for cowards! Go the full distance! Give it everything you got! DON'T QUIT! And when you've been given an extra five minutes, don't waste that opportunity, and give THAT everything you got too! PUSH PAST YOUR LIMITS! Go the extra mile! And THEN some! Then marvel at how far you've gone, smile, and tell yourself you can do it again...

MAINTAIN AWARENESS

We spend so much of our efforts focused on mission success sometimes that very often people forget to check their surroundings. Just when things are going their best, that's often the ripest opportunity for disaster to strike. So, when the path ahead looks bright and sunny, when the world is peachy and everything seems to be going exactly according to plan, check six... You may have just fallen into a preventable trap, and you might never know it until it's too late...

"Complacency kills", as the old aviation adage goes, and it will readily destroy your chances of being successful just the same. While we work to reach our goals, we should never forget to remain vigilant of potential threats along the way - and not only just for ourselves, but for our teams, our sections, and our organizations alike as well. If we ever want to accomplish the mission, to achieve success, to reach our goals, we have an individual responsibility to keep our head on a swivel and look out for stumbling blocks in our path. We have an obligation to be proactive, not reactive, and to mitigate, plan for contingencies, and/or even to engage threats as we identify them when necessary.

Some people will happily skip through life completely oblivious to the potentials looming on the horizon, and when disaster strikes, will be caught off-guard, blindsided, and more than likely, cry they never saw it coming... Well, the fact of the matter is, they didn't. But they could have, and that's the point. Don't ever allow yourself to become so fixated on the goal that you forget to be mindful of your surroundings. Letting yourself fall into a routine will surely create a false sense of security, and while you're zeroed in on the task at hand, you're almost guaranteed to miss all that is happening around you, and with it, miss potential dangers when they approach.

Today, take some time to consider past times you may have fallen into the trap of blindly focusing on a goal. Fascination/Fixation is a visual illusion that can happen to anyone, and it most often occurs when we have become complacent due to comfortability with the routine of our daily lives. It is in this moment, when we're too comfortable with our ability to perform the job, that we're susceptible to blindly pursuing a goal... And it is in that moment, when we're not paying attention to everything else happening around us, that we miss noticing a potential disaster fast approaching us.

If you ever find that you've become fixated on the goal, stop and pull back for a second... Take a moment to understand what's happening, let someone else take over the controls for a minute, and reevaluate the situation... You just might discover something you missed, you might catch a mistake previously overlooked, and you might save yourself from a preventable trap... Keep the watch, and never assume that, because the winds are fair, the seas are too. We must remember to remain vigilant. Otherwise... You might become a target, and when you do... You'll have no one to blame for the wreckage you find yourself in but yourself.

PREPARE FOR WHAT YOU CAN'T SEE COMING

It is exceedingly rare to see the very edge of a storm. Normally, storms engulf you before you realize it. Even raging hurricanes have a way of creeping up on you, starting with a slight drizzle and a minor breeze... Then before long, torrential rain and high winds are barring down upon you. It's rare to see the front of trouble as it heads your way. Indeed, throughout most of our lives, issues and problems, stress and fatigue, hardships and adversity will come at you like a hurricane... Slowly, and with overwhelming force. Yet you can survive just fine if you're well-trained and well-prepared.

People who spend time preparing diligently for the possibility of upcoming storms find it easier to weather those storms when they occur. People who have trained themselves to respond appropriately to impending disasters tend to thrive during those events when they happen. Just because you're no longer out at sea, doesn't mean you'll no longer encounter these things. The only difference between the storms at sea and the storms on the mountain is the manner in which they form, but make no mistake, freezing temperatures, cold winds, and heavy snow will kill you all the same. This is why, before you even started your climb, you should have prepared for the possibility of these events and packed your ruck with appropriate supplies.

Like the storms that creep up on us, the storms of our lives can be handled just fine with proper training and preparation. Learning what causes stress can help you find forms of stress relief. Learning how to think around problems and listening to understand others can lead to solutions. Seeing hardships and adversity as opportunities for growth and development can increase personal resiliency, define good character, and create strength. And understanding that there's always room for improvement helps maintain the humility required for continuous learning to take place.

Today's a day to focus on preparing for the storms you'll likely encounter as you press on ahead, but that you may not ever see coming while climbing the mountain. Through getting an understanding of the mission and its requirements, learning about the path ahead and the checkpoints you'll need to reach, and taking into account the environment and likely dangers you'll come across along the way, you can plan contingencies, train and prepare to handle emergencies, and face problems as they creep up upon you.

It's rare to see a storm coming at you. Most often they tend to creep up on us, and before we realize what's happening, we're right in the middle of it all, dealing with the many problems it brought with it. But if you focus on continuous growth and development, preparedness and training, the little ones won't be a problem at all, and you'll learn to handle the big ones that creep up on you as well. All that'll be left is maintaining the right attitude, and before you know it, the storm will have passed, and you'll be standing tall on the other side.

MITIGATE RISK

Potential hazards loom on the horizon every day, lying in wait, biding their time until the right time to strike. They could come in a rock fall, a surge of strong winds, a microburst, or a heavy snowstorm. They might happen due to failure of the weakening lines no one has been inspecting, or a missed hazard the fatigued watch, who's now sleeping, missed spotting because they haven't been properly relieved by their late replacement, or the loose straps that weren't properly secured and haven't been checked since... There's risk inherently present in any journey, but ask yourself this... Should the knowledge of their potential existence keep you from pressing on?

Let's face facts here... You don't walk out the door in the morning believing for a second no dangers exist. The drive to work has the potential to be hazardous due to weather conditions and human factors (like distracted and aggressive drivers), your workplace may be filled with potential hazards (like heights, confined spaces, falling objects, and more), and conducting daily operations may inevitably involve navigating an onslaught of hazardous conditions, objects, and errors too numerous to list here. Regardless of what your profession is, it's conceivable that you're well aware of the potential risks involved in the path you chose... So why do people seem to believe whenever a risk presents itself that suddenly everything needs to grind to a halt?

You have a job to do, and life needs to happen. Things will progress and the world will continue to spin whether you take the next step forward or not. The mission doesn't change just because there's risk involved, and as such, we shouldn't stop operations just because we discover a hazard along the way either... No. We train for those things, we plan for them, and we work to mitigate their potential for occurrence and degree of threat if they raise their head, but we don't stop moving forward because we know they're out there. Good leaders learn to accept risk as a natural part of the mission, and then properly mitigate them through training, planning, and preparedness.

You're taking a life-altering journey across a vast expanse of open sea filled with storms, ultimately navigating toward a mountain that reaches beyond sight! What were you expecting, a pleasure cruise?!

Today, spend some time contemplating the risks you encounter in your daily life... Do you account for them? Do you plan for them? Do you train for their possibility? Do you, your team, and your organization put controls in place to mitigate them to an acceptable level and move forward with reaching the goal(s)? Think about it... You've committed to arguably the hardest life-long endeavor possible, there's bound to be risks along the way. Don't let their possibility become an anchor that prevents you from moving forward. You'll never be successful if you can't learn to properly mitigate the risks you already know you'll encounter along the way, accept the fact that you'll inevitably encounter them, and make the decision to continue on with the mission at hand.

BE FLEXIBLE ALONG YOUR JOURNEY

The journey to your success in life is a lot like traveling. It takes time, careful planning, a desire for adventure, staying positive when things don't go according to plan, some adaptability, a willingness to learn new things, and much, much more. Sometimes things won't go as planned, sometimes it will be lonely, sometimes there might be a bit of danger, and quite often it will be seriously hard work to get where you want to go... But all that is what makes the journey worth it, and on the other side, you'll become far better, stronger, more capable, and wiser due to those experiences.

If you consider all of these things, it's easy to understand why those people who can adapt easily to changing situations and environments have a stronger desire to travel to new places than those who lack flexibility, and an easier time reaching new destinations than those who are rigid in their thinking and problem-solving. Problems will inevitably arise in even the best laid-out plans, and whether those problems are major or minor, your ability to be flexible and adapt to the situation at hand will ultimately determine your success at making it to your intended destination in one piece or not. No journey is without challenge, and the best travelers are able to think on their feet to overcome those challenges. Thus, people who can remain flexible, positive, and adaptable in the face of challenges disrupting their plans, tend to enjoy taking journeys more than those who lack these traits.

Like globetrotting, your own personal developmental journey also requires flexibility and adaptability. Your climb up the mountain will be met with obstacles and blockades, loose rocks and thin ledges, high winds and steep cliffs... Even your best planning won't prepare you for those times when the unexpected strikes and you're forced to change course, adjust, or even alter your perspective in order to solve problems and continue moving forward. Despite all the training, planning, and preparation in the world, you need to remain flexible along your journey if you're ever going to reach your goals.

Today, take some time to reflect on your ability to remain flexible and adaptable in the face of changing situations. Start by understanding that there is no "set path" that you have to stick to in order to be successful in your life. What may have worked for one person may not work for another. One person's climb may be too difficult for you to replicate, and the path another person already carved might no longer be available... Your journey is your journey, not theirs, and as such, you're making it up as you go. You have a chance to blaze a new trail no one has ever taken before, but in doing so, you must learn to identify challenges when you encounter them and make changes to yourself and your plans in order to overcome them and achieve success.

Don't be afraid to change direction if you find the path you're currently on too perilous to proceed... There are solutions to the problems you encounter all around you. They might be a different handhold, a different type of teamwork, or a different path altogether. Your ability to identify the challenge is only half the battle... Your ability to be flexible through adaptation and changing your approach to overcome those challenge is the other.

CLIMBING A MOUNTAIN

For what purpose do we climb a mountain? Is it to see the world from the top? Is it just to reach the top? Is it simply because it's there? Or is there something up there we need? What paths do we take while climbing a mountain? Do we head directly toward the top? Are we able to walk an already cleared path? Are we forced to carve our own? Or do we plan our direction according to the situation? What does it take to climb a mountain? Is it simply putting one foot in front of the other? Must we call on some courage to face fears along the way? Should we train for endurance as well as strength? Or is our deep-dwelling, internalized motivation enough to see us through?

The truth is, climbing a mountain is an exercise in leadership, and it requires Purpose, Direction, and Motivation to make it to the top. We need a reason to start the journey, we need to know how we're going to get there, and those things can fuel our motivation to train, prepare, embark, and when all efforts have been spent, press on. But after a while, it's easy to forget why we started the journey in the first place. After all, there won't always be a clear path, and our goals may change over time... Staying stagnant in the valley won't improve our lives and doing nothing is the best way to guarantee you'll never reach your goals.

Now, you may be asking yourself, "what does YOU climbing a mountain have to do with leadership?!" Well... "Leadership" is "The ability to provide purpose, direction, and motivation, while operating to accomplish the mission, and improve the organization."... And if you start your climb up your mountain, you'll be striving to reach new goals through the process of self-improvement. Simply taking the journey will show others around you that it can be done, that reaching the goal is possible. And while you're making your climb on the path to personal self-betterment, you'll be able to look back, and I guarantee you'll notice people following in the footsteps you've laid down along the way. Congratulations... Your efforts to climb a mountain just lead others to do the same... You're a leader by example, so you NEED to set the RIGHT example, and remember why you're there, lest you lead them down a dangerous path...

So far, you've been taking the journey to climb a mountain with no summit... A never-ending journey of personal growth and self-improvement. You have a reason for embarking on this endeavor, and identified a direction to reach your goals... And this has given you the motivation to endure all the adversity and hardship you've encountered along the way... But many who embark upon this journey, at some point along the way, forget why they're on the side of a mountain in the first place... It's easy to lose sight of our purpose in the processes of striving to reach our goals... Therefore, today is a great time to stop and reflect on all the reasons you have for climbing this mountain in the first place... Do you still have the same purpose and the same goals after all this time? Are you still heading in the same direction and are you still just as motivated today as you were when you first started?

If you find you're having trouble clearly articulating the answers to these questions, that's ok! Spend some time reflecting and rediscover those answers once again! Find a purpose, pick a direction, be motivated, and climb your mountain! You might just lead others to success along the way... If you do, you'll be living THE definition of Leadership by virtue of your efforts, and you'll find your goals easier to reach.

LIFE IS AN ADVENTURE

Life is an adventure. Your job is to live it to the fullest. Your mission, to cross the finish line accomplished, successful, remembered, surrounded by loving friends and family, and filled to the hilt with experiences...

At some point in everyone's life, we come to a crossroads, and we have a choice... An easy path and a difficult path stand at our feet. The easy path leads us nowhere special. Looking down the way, you'll find a well-paved road leading to a life of convenience, where no risk is required, no effort need be expended, and the rewards are just as mediocre and disappointing as the life lived by the people who have chosen to walk it...

On the other hand, the difficult path is filled with unknown hardships and unknown possibilities alike. The path is narrow and not very clear and leads up a seemingly impossibly high mountain with no end in sight. At times it seems to completely disappear, and there are significant obstacles along what might be the way. Yet far off in the distance, and high up on that mountain, you can just barely make out meaningful rewards achieved by highly admirable individuals whose lives have been a story filled with adventure, experiences, and triumph...

The journey to success, the path to greatness, the road to achievement, is only possible to find along the difficult path. It's the one filled with experiences beyond imagination, but sadly, most people who arrive at the crossroad of their life take one look at that difficult path, then choose the easy path. If that's what you want for your life, then feel free to take that path and be just like everyone else... But keep in mind, that road is crowded.

Just stop and think for a moment... You have only ONE life to live! Your time here is limited, and every second you waste NOT making progress toward achieving your dreams is time you basically threw down the drain! Your life is SUPPOSED to be an adventure! It's a cup waiting to be filled with amazing experiences, relationships, and worthy accomplishments! Don't choose the wide, easy path... Don't be like the sheep-filled crowd. Choose the hard path that you'll often have to carve yourself and be exceptional!

Today's a day to stop and remember why you chose the hard path in the first place. Taking the hard path practically guarantees a difficult road ahead in life, but the reward is answering the call of adventure beckoning you from afar. Sure... At times the journey may be harsh, agonizing, and lonely... But at other times it may be fun, it may be enjoyable, and it may be glorious... You may not see the goal, and the end may not be in sight, the finish line may appear impossibly far... But you can make it... You only need to remind yourself you can. After all, the only assurance that you'll never reach the goal, is giving up.

So, take the hard path up the seemingly impossibly high mountain! Why? BECAUSE LIFE IS AN ADVENTURE! And your job is to live it to the fullest! Choose NOT to be mediocre, but exceptional in the face of surrounding unprecedented mediocrity. And during your journey to achieve success in life, may I make a simple suggestion for you to keep in mind while you're traveling along? Don't forget to stop and admire all that is around you with frequent regularity... You'll thank me someday. I guarantee it.

CHOOSE EXCEPTIONALISM

It is our unfortunate reality that we live in a world filled to the hilt with unprecedented mediocrity. A world where underachievement and half-hearted efforts are hailed by a generation as "something worthy of praise", and a culture of sheeple glance over REAL achievement while dismissing, ridiculing, and sometimes shunning it as a standard set too high for social acceptance to tolerate. We live in a society where fewer and fewer individuals truly shine above the rest in their accomplishment of great and meaningful things, all because fewer are willing to strive to climb the mountain while most simply believe they are entitled to the rewards without the effort to attain them...

But ALL have a CHOICE in life. One day everyone will come to their crossroads and gaze out upon the wide and the narrow paths, and each will have a decision to make. You can choose to be soft, weak, self-entitled, lazy, dependent, and pathetic. OR... You can choose to be hardcore, work your butt off, learn from hardship and adversity, overcome all odds, and truly make something of yourself worthy of admiration, respect, and meaningful praise! In our day and age, to willingly choose to break apart from the rest and strike out on your own path is to make a conscious decision toward seeking exceptionalism in life. And to all those on the overly crowded streets of mediocrity far below you, who catch a glimpse of what you earned and cry with envy "It's not fair", I got news for them... You're NOT "entitled" to ANYTHING in life, and that even includes life itself...

There's no such thing as "fair" and no one is guaranteed a "tomorrow". If you waste your life following the crowd while merely dreaming of "something better", it will never happen, and you'll eventually find your life wasted and filled with regret at unrealized "dreams". Therefore, if you aren't willing to do something TODAY, to use what you have to your advantage TODAY, to improve yourself TODAY, then I don't want to hear a single word out of your mouth about your woes tomorrow. The exceptionalism of one does not equal the loss of another. But an individual's refusal to part with mediocrity will hold them back, prevent their progress, poison their efforts, and ruin their chances at attaining their hopes and dreams.

You've been on your climb for quite a while now, and looking back below, you've discovered you've reached unprecedented heights! You can see the mediocre masses far below, stuck in the valley merely dreaming of success in their self-entitled moans, while your team is hot on your heels seeking improvement right along with you... Today, make a conscious decision to reaffirm your commitment to a life of exceptionalism! Let your progress thus far fuel your motivation to strive on! The air's getting thin up here but give the day everything you got! Hit the ground running every single day! Grow despite adversity, if anything IN SPITE of adversity, and make something of yourself truly worthy of praise! REFUSE to be just like the sheep who praise themselves and pat themselves on the back for their own mediocrity. No... You're BETTER than that! Hold yourself and your team to ever-increasingly higher standards! YOUR dreams are within your reach! You only need to strive for them.

ATTITUDE MAKES ALL THE DIFFERENCE

"There's a time and place for all things", so the saying goes... And while I largely ascribe to this saying, I firmly attest that there is never not a time for a positive attitude. "Positivity" is infectious, and the right attitude can "make" any situation. The world around you may seem to be falling apart, but with a positive attitude, you can find the silver lining that sees you through... The endeavor before you may appear daunting and full of peril, but with the right attitude, you can rise to meet the challenge and overcome... The race may seem hopelessly long and the competition difficult at best, but with a positive attitude, you can beat the odds and win the day...

They say a diatribe is no friend to success, and pessimism can bring ruin and defeat, even when the goal is within your grasp... So, no matter the situation, regardless of the company, despite all odds, and whatever the time and wherever the place may be... A positive attitude is always appropriate, and it can mean the difference between greatness and success, or agony and defeat.

Understand this... Your journey to success in life will be the hardest thing you'll ever undertake. As you've experienced by now, the exhaustingly long hours, the physical and mental pain and stress, the setbacks and roadblocks, barriers and hurdles to overcome, and the never-ending problems and issues you'll face, all will challenge the core of your being and the very depths of your soul. But let me tell you a secret...

With the "right" attitude... You've already won. All YOU need to do is show up!

Ninety percent of being successful at life is simply just showing up! Be in the right place, at the right time, and in the right uniform, and you've already achieved a measure of success! Doing your job is the remaining ten percent and having the "right" attitude about it all makes that extra ten that puts you over the top... 110%. Simply just look at all you've achieved so far! Where are you right now in your journey?! THAT'S RIGHT! You're on top of a mountain! You can see the curvature of the Earth itself! The sky has never been a deeper shade of blue, the sun so blindingly bright, and the air so crisp! You can't even see the far-off land where your journey first began you've come so far! And what got you here? Exactly what was it that allowed you to even consider taking that first step off the shores of that beach?

A POSITIVE ATTITUDE! That's what it was!

Attitude can make or break ANY situation! So today, just take a few moments to reflect on your attitude so far since you first started... I guarantee there have been days where you're attitude sucked! Where pessimism began creeping in, complaints rolled off the tongue, and bitterness and anger at a situation or two filled your thoughts... Don't deny it! We're all human after all. Accept it, embrace it, learn from it, and make a conscious effort to remember what came after! I'll also wager money that bad attitude didn't improve the situation at the time either, did it? There's a time and place for all things... But it's NEVER a bad time for a positive attitude. With the right attitude, you've already won... So, lead yourself, and your team, to show up and win the day. After all, with the right attitude, the rest is easy.

CAPSTONE DAYS

THERE'S NO SUCH THING AS A "LEADERSHIP EXPERT"

There exist all kinds of approaches to leadership, too many applications to count, far too many personality traits, and so many theories on the subject they could fill a library... And with that being said, let's get something straight...

There is no such thing as a "Leadership Expert".

"Leadership" is a dynamic process and "Leadership Development" is a never-ending, self-motivated, individual endeavor toward self-betterment. As a science, no amount of money spent on lessons, no number of books read, no amount of time spent listening to someone talk on stage, and no proclaimed (self or not) "expert", will EVER be able to teach YOU to BE a leader. The simple fact of the matter is, that there are no "secrets", no "10 tricks", and no "special knowledge" that will help you become a leader either. Despite all the junk media you'll find in hoards online attempting to entice you with keywords, or all the college professors who profess opinions, the ONLY person capable of developing YOU, is YOU... And it is in the self-motivated act of personal development that we find leadership development possible.

Be cautious of people who approach you and claim to be experts, who claim they have all the wisdom, and that they can teach you to be a leader. No one can "teach" you to "be" a leader. You can learn all the theories, case studies, techniques, and practices in the world... But no one can ever make you into a person capable of leadership for you... That's something only YOU can do for yourself, and to get there, you have to WANT to do it. In your self-motivated journey to do so, you'll quickly discover it's an uphill climb to scale a mountain with no summit, and that your journey has no end, meaning no matter how high you've climbed, you'll ALWAYS have room for more growth.

THIS is exactly why there's no such thing as an "expert" to leadership! Because AS a "dynamic" and "never-ending" process, there's always more to learn and more possibilities than any supposed "expert" can possibly fathom! Just when the world's leading individuals seem to have it all figured out, BOOM! The dynamic changes!

Today, take time to contemplate the nature of this concept... That there truly are no living experts to leadership. The act of "leading" is possible both with and without anyone to lead. It's the purposeful act of climbing your mountain daily and willfully seeking out continuous growth. As you do so, you'll find your capability and capacity for leadership increases, and the influence you are capable of imparting along with it. Anyone who tells you they can give you the "secrets" to these things or tell you the "tricks" to "be" a leader of ANY kind, is both a liar and is trying to sell you something. Someone can show you how to get there, and someone can lead you up the mountain... But it is you, and ONLY you, who is capable of growing yourself, and therefore it is you, and only you, who is capable of making yourself into the leader you desire to become.

NO ONE DEFINITION FOR SUCCESS

I'm sure you've heard the illustration before... Thomas Edison failed a hundred times before successfully making the incandescent light bulb, yet the truth is, it wasn't that he "failed" a hundred times up to that point, but instead, that he simply found a hundred ways how NOT to make the bulb... The implication here is that, as long as you keep trying, you will eventually succeed. However, there's another implication we can draw from Edison's success story...

Since that time, we've created tons of new light bulbs, powered through tons of different energy sources, and that work through tons of new methodologies utilizing technologies previously non-existent. Therefore, a far better implication exists, which is that successfully producing a light bulb can be achieved through any number of a growing list of possibilities no one knew about previously until some bold innovator tried and was eventually successful in their endeavors. The reality is that, while there may be a million wrong paths that will prevent you from reaching the goal, this fact in no way implies that it is only possible for one correct path to exist.

The truth of the matter is, an unknown number of possibilities exist for you to achieve success in life, most of which haven't even been tried or discovered yet. However, the prevailing message in our society, and even within our educational systems, is that there's only one "right answer" to success. While this logic may apply directly to things like math and history, it doesn't apply logically to human factors in producing achievement. Just because one person managed to reach a goal one way, doesn't mean that's the only way possible for you to reach the same goal. You may not be capable of replicating what someone else achieved in the way they achieved it, but that doesn't mean you can't achieve the same thing in a different way in which you are capable of.

Today, take some time to consider if you've confined yourself to the belief that only one path exists, that maybe you've convinced yourself that there is only one definition for the success you dream of. If you're ever going to be successful in your endeavors, learn to think outside the box. Don't allow yourself to be confined to a singular set of possibilities as the only methodologies for reaching your goals. Most often we'll hit roadblocks and completely fail to notice another potential path exists that can allow us to keep moving forward, and the best way to remove the mental blinders that prevent us from discovering those new paths is by removing the idea that "success" can only be defined one way from our mentalities.

There is no "one definition" to producing success in life, and it's once we realize and understand this, that we discover a universe of new possibilities to successfully make our light bulbs are all around us. Edison's example teaches us that success is possible by not giving up, sure, but history teaches us that his path wasn't the only possible way to achieve the same success either. Knowing this, don't lock yourself into thinking there's only one path to reach your goals. You may simply have yet to discover any of a million possible paths to achieve success.

LIVE IN THE REAL WORLD

Why do you even care what others are doing or not doing? Why do you waste your time, hours on end, flicking your finger across a stupid screen? How do any of those useless stories, opinions, or videos help you?

The sad truth is, that the overwhelmingly vast majority of it all does nothing but waste your time...

Time is your most precious resource! You only have so much of it, and just think of all the time - YOUR time - you've thrown away wrapped up in things so beyond meaningless and worthless to your REAL life. You will NEVER get that time back! And you will NEVER make something of yourself by focusing your attention on the lives of others or embedded within a fake existence on a screen. "Success" and "Achievement" are TANGIBLE things attained by physical efforts! So, stop throwing away your time and START focusing on your own "here" and "now".

Ask yourself... What have you done, physically today, to help you reach your goals? If you find the answer is, "Nothing because I've wasted those precious moments staring at a worthless screen, living in the hopes and dreams of someone else, fuming at the comments and opinionated opinions of others..." Then I've got some bad news for you... You just threw away a day of your life in the garbage. Your life is worth more than some stupid screen, some stupid social media feed, some ignorant opinions, or someone else's car, house, money, or adventure! Stop wasting your life paying attention to all that and LIVE! Your focus should be spent on improving your OWN life! Become something MORE than you were yesterday.

Because THAT is the only way you will ever get where you want to go in life!

Today is a challenge. Today, you're required to live an entire 24 hours WITHOUT spending a single second on ANY social media platform, playing ANY phone or computer games, reading ANY comics or leisure type material, or doing any activity that is NOT productive to your own self-improvement. THAT is the challenge. Today, focus entirely on simply living in the REAL world and paying attention to the "here and now". Real life isn't all cupcakes, butterflies, and rainbows... We KNOW this by now, right?! It's a cold, hard, harsh reality, sure, but getting after your dreams and living life to the fullest is FAR better than hibernating in some dark room sitting in front of a screen merely dreaming of success while wasting your hours away wallowing in the fake existence of others. Social media and digital existences are more addictive than drugs, and if you're not careful, you'll eventually discover you've wasted thousands of hours of the only time you'll ever have on this Earth accomplishing NOTHING.

Why do you care what other people have to say on the internet anyway? Most comments are just opinions and most opinions are uneducated and unintelligent anti-intellectual garbage anyway. YOU have a real opportunity to live an amazing life, and you're letting a fake existence take that from you? Don't! Get up, get out, stand up tall, look the world boldly in the face, and set out on your journey... THAT is the only way you'll ever achieve your dreams.

CHANGE YOURSELF

If you want to make an impact in the world, you must first allow yourself to be impacted. If you want to make a change in the world, you must first allow yourself to be changed. If you want to lead, you must first learn to follow...

Notice a pattern here?

We can't demand the world to change just because we don't like something or don't agree with something, no more than we can force other people to change their beliefs just because we don't agree with them. People who refuse to accept this reality are often compared to standing at a cliff's edge, screaming at the world in the distance to change while shaking their fists. The world won't change just because you don't like the way it is. The world doesn't care what you think, and in the face of the world, you're insignificant. The world is far bigger than you, older than you, and will be around long after you're gone, and before you can accomplish anything meaningful in your life, you need to come to accept that fact.

If you REALLY want to drive change, make an impact, and lead others down a better path, then stop focusing on the world, and START focusing on yourself. A belief that you can forcefully change something you have zero control over is an act of stupidity, so why do so many people scream and cry about the world when their focus SHOULD be on something they can actually control? Refusing to point fingers and starting to hold yourself accountable instead is an act of finally learning to take acceptance of personal responsibility for your life. It's only when you come to terms with the idea that you can't change the world, but you can change yourself, that you can finally begin to make a difference.

It's far too easy for us to become wrapped up in focusing on all the injustices, wrongs, and evils of the world. Yet the problem is, no matter how much you scream at the world, the world won't change just because you cry over its evils and injustices. The reality of life is, you have zero control over the world, but complete control over yourself, and THAT is where you'll find your greatest opportunity to produce change and make a real impact.

Today, take some time to consider how leading by example produces change in the world around you as a result. Think about it... The world isn't responsible for your problems, you are. As such, why do you waste your time pointing fingers when you could see real improvement if you simply focused on improving yourself? If you want to change the world around you, stop focusing on the world's faults, and start working to improve upon your own instead. BE the example you want to see in the world, and as you begin to grow yourself, you'll notice the world around you slowly start to change as a result. Stop demanding other people to change for you, and instead, lead by example, and what you'll be amazed to find, is that some of the world will follow the example you set.

GROW YOUR TOTAL SELF

Psalm 28:7 (KJV) - "The LORD is my strength and my shield; my heart trusted in him, and I am helped: therefore, my heart greatly rejoiceth; and with my song will I praise him."

"Strength" comes in many forms... There's the most obvious, physical strength (cardiovascular fitness, muscular strength, endurance, diet, a strong immune system, and overall wellness), but there's also mental strength (resilience, tenacity, perseverance, education, intellectual growth, and intestinal fortitude), strength of character (Loyalty, Duty, Respect, Selfless Service, Honor, Integrity, and Personal Courage), and even strength of spirit (Faith in God).

Merely focusing on building strength in one or two areas simply isn't good enough for a true warrior and a true leader, you must focus on constantly improving in all areas you can. To be victorious in combat you need strength of body, strength of mind, strength of character, and strength of spirit, and to be successful in life is no different. Don't merely focus on just one or two areas while ignoring the rest and believe all will be ok. Your growth should ALWAYS encompass your total self. As the old saying goes, "a chain is only as strong as its weakest link..." So, let not one link of your chain remain weak.

Of course, your journey to build strength begins with recognizing that room for improvement exists, but a failure to recognize – or even to admit – that you have more than merely one or two areas you're capable of growing is practically setting yourself up for defeat. You don't plan on going into an engagement against an enemy weak-willed, undertrained, under-equipped, and unprepared... No, you don't. You build a team with the right people for the right jobs, train and equip them to the fullest, build morale and plan for every contingency, and engage KNOWING you'll be victorious! Your team is your strength, and while each position may focus on different areas and specialties all their own, they work together as one to accomplish the mission. To make the best team possible, each member must be trained to their maximum potential, otherwise, they might fail.

Just like the strength your well-trained, high-performance team brings to the fight, your own personal success comes as a result of developing your total self to be the strongest it can be too. Regardless of physical, mental, spiritual, or your character, all aspects of your life should be included in your continuous developmental process. To overlook or willingly let one area go without is to ignore a vitally important capability, that without, could cost you the battle. Why would you do that to yourself?!

Today, take some time to consider if you've been focused on ONLY developing some areas of your total self while overlooking or completely ignoring others. If you find this to be the case, next ask yourself, would you go into a firefight without a Medic? What about without your gunner? How about without Commo? Ops? Terp? Demo? Supply? Proper equipment, intel, and/or a plan? If you answered no to those things, next ask yourself... Why then are you not developing all areas of your team (self)? Without those things, you're begging to lose the engagement, just like without growing all areas of yourself possible, you're begging to fail at leadership. Grow your total self... Your success, and the success of your team, depends on it.

TRAPPED IN A FOG

Have you ever felt as if you were stuck in a fog? As if the road ahead has become difficult to see and you can't tell where you're going? Like a creeping air of uncertainty has made the journey of your life feel ambiguous at best? It happens to us all at one point or another. Sometimes we have a plan, but someone or something is holding us back. Sometimes our path was made unclear when circumstances created chaos in our life. And sometimes, some people simply walk themselves in circles, never clearly having direction in the first place.

A foggy existence can cloud your purpose and direction, and to be successful you need both. Knowing and understanding this, we all have a choice to make. We can choose to allow others to dictate our path, to let circumstances force our direction, to claim we can't move forward because we can't see the way, and remain lost as makers of our own demise... Or we can take charge of our fate and find a way to keep moving forward.

No one ever said you would always know the way to go in life, but so long as you keep moving forward, eventually, you'll clear the fog. Unsuccessful people hold on tightly to that "victim" card and remain lost in a fog with no clear purpose, direction, or motivation in their lives. They'll blame anyone and anything else for the fact that they're lost and have fallen short in life. Anyone and anything, that is, but themselves. And since they don't believe anyone can teach them anything, and they have no room for improvement, they'll continue to walk in circles while unjustly claiming the world is somehow responsible for all their self-imposed problems.

But successful people strive to find a positive path to reach their goals. Successful people are constantly evaluating themselves for improvement, and this includes keeping tabs on their progress as well. They outline their plan, make clearly defined goals, and mark off when they've cleared checkpoints along the way. Successful people can recognize when they're not making the progress they're shooting for, or when they've deviated from their intended path. They know when they've become trapped in a fog, and since they're not finger-pointing, self-imposed victims, they take well-planned action to get back on track.

Today, take some time to consider the possibilities of unknowingly getting trapped in a fog. It can happen to the best of us. If you ever find your future without clear direction, next you should be asking yourself if you're lost. It very well may be the case that you are, and you may not know what to do or where to go next. That's ok! What's important when that time comes is deciding for yourself if you're the maker of your fate or a victim of circumstance. The decision is ultimately yours, but know this... The only people who make it out of foggy existences and go on to make something successful of themselves in life are those who recognized the need to grow beyond their circumstances. It is impossible to be a victim and be successful at the same time.

CASTLES

Castles are intriguing architectural marvels of beauty and design that, throughout history, have served as physical representations of both progress and conflict. As human civilizations advanced through the ages, so did the systems that ruled over and governed the population - for the better or worse. As rulers gained more power and prominence and were able to exert influence over increasing expanses, more and more challenges to their position would spring up.

Conflict would arise from those who didn't want to be controlled, or who wanted power for themselves, or by those who felt they weren't being treated fairly and justly, or any of a hundred other reasons. And so, castles became a physical form of protection against outside threats, to protect the leaders, safeguard wealth, and to act as a centralized location of governance. Often carved and built of the strongest materials possible, they provided a home, a form of defense, a capital, and a repository for knowledge, supplies, medicine, and much more... Often immaculately decorated and meticulously designed, great detail and craftsmanship poured into every aspect, they took years, and decades to construct, and they can last for ages on end if cared for properly.

Yet a whole new problem arises as kingdoms advance and influence grows... Castles, it seems, tend to become prisons for the rulers who inhabit them. It isn't difficult for rulers of a castle to spend a lifetime trapped within the well-decorated and well-built walls they've erected around themselves. Shut off from experiencing the very world they rule over; their influence becomes limited and the growth of their kingdom stagnates. And exactly like the act of building a castle to serve a kingdom, the act of bettering yourself and exerting leadership can create the need for erecting a castle within yourself too.

As you advance and exert influence, the number of threats you'll encounter to yourself, your position, your well-being, and indeed your very identity, increases along with it. It's all too easy for us to respond by building fortresses within ourselves - mentally speaking - to protect ourselves from such threats, but few people realize that this can turn into a trap preventing them from making any kind of progress at all. As we erect walls within ourselves to protect us from those who would lay siege upon us, we effectively begin to shut ourselves off from others who are important to us. Like those rulers of expansive kingdoms who yet can never leave the castle walls, we too become detached leaders who can never leave the walls we use to keep others out.

We become birds in a cage of our own making, trapped and unable to fly free.

Today, take some time to consider the castle you've built within yourself. We all have one. It's our defense mechanism and internal protections we've erected against attacking hoards. Has your castle shut you off from your team, friends, or family? Has your castle stagnated your growth? Castles are amazing marvels of beauty and design, and well-cared for, they can withstand the tolls of time... But they can also become cages that prevent us from growing beyond a certain point. A wise leader knows how to rule in such a way that the castle - while necessary - remains open and accessible to their kingdom. As such, in order to avoid being trapped inside your own castle, learn to treat those around you with care so you may avoid becoming closed off for the sake of your own protection, and forced into stagnation due to the restriction of growth you've now created for yourself.

DECOMPRESS FROM STRESS

Stress can come from many sources, can be either physical or mental, and can be both positive and negative. Physical stress and stressors generally build up quickly, so they're easy to see, but mental stress builds up slowly over time without us ever realizing it until it takes its toll on us. Yet, of the two, mental stress is often negative, and it's also the one we most often create for ourselves...

People stress over nearly everything these days, don't they? In a world filled with pressure from all sides trying to force your choices, judgmental ignorance trying to tear you down, lies and bias, hate and malice, corruption and just pure evil... People CHOOSE to stress over all the things in the world that they simply have no control over.

Why do you do that to yourselves?

There will always be another "wrong" in the world, another injustice, another conflict, another fight... Unless any of it involves you directly, why would you choose to allow any of that to become a part of your life? Eventually, every person will come to understand that the world is filled with injustices, but that doesn't mean you have any obligation to get involved and weigh you down. You have to learn to let go of the dead weight needlessly adding stress into your life.

They say a warrior must quiet the mind, and calm the heart and soul, in order to master their craft. Being a warrior in a garden requires calming of the self so as not to destroy the peace around you. If you are corrupted by negative stresses, it will reflect outwardly, and the turbulence of the mind and heart will become the wrath of the body. Your garden will be destroyed by a storm of your own making, and that's the reality for those who choose to allow the negative stress of the world to poison their lives.

Today, take some time to simply stop and think deeply about all the different stressors you have in your life. Physical stress – such as work and exercise – are essential to a healthy life and physical fitness, but the majority of mental stress is nothing more than self-imposed useless dead weight you're choosing to carry around. If you let the problems of the world invade your life and waste your time, you'll soon find those very things are what's holding you back.

Drop the dead weight of needless stress in your life. You don't need to care about all the things you can't control in the world. We can only carry so much... We only have two hands. The weight of the world and all its problems are too much for anyone. Instead, focus on your own life – your issues, your family and friends, your team and organization, your growth and success. Learn to quiet your mind and calm your soul. Turn your focus every day on bettering yourself and let go of all the useless stress you're allowing to weigh you down, and I promise you, your world around you, and your life, will be significantly less stressful, and significantly better for it.

CHERISH YOUR LIFE

If you woke up this morning and watched the sunrise... First of all, you should have been thankful to even do so... But second, ask yourself, do you understand the journey that light had to go through just for you to enjoy the moment you experienced watching it? The light you're seeing traveled 92.96 million miles through the void of space just to be here. Did you know that? It traveled at 300,000 km/sec and took 8 minutes and 20 seconds just to be here, present, in that very moment, for you to enjoy the beauty of life this morning.

What we're seeing when we watch a sunrise is merely a fraction of the whole spectrum of light, and it's the "leftovers" at that. It's the stuff that didn't get absorbed or reflected by something else along the way. The remainder that survived the perils of open space, intense gravitational forces, magnetic waves, dust, debris, and everything in our atmosphere, to be able to make its way to you, pass through the tiny opening in your eyes, hit your fovea, activate your cones, and generate signals to your brain. The small amount of energy carried with it is directly responsible for continued life on this planet, and the mere suggestion that it's a truly beautiful sight to see doesn't even fully capture the magnitude of the moment...

The average person in our age might be able to witness roughly 30,000 sunrises in their lifetime, and each one is unique. From one passing moment to the next, no two are ever the same. The one you watched this morning, that exact moment, has never happened before in all of history, it will never happen again, and the captured image in your memories or on a photograph (if you took one) will in no way do the moment justice either. Our journey through life is a series of moments that have never happened before and will never happen again. They are all unique in some way, and it's truly a blessing that we get to experience them.

Yet many people curse the sunrise and the morning. Many people don't appreciate the beauty of the moment they bring and can't find it within themselves to understand why they should. Far too often do people ignore these moments, dismiss them as mundane, and take them for granted due to a perceived normalcy in their occurrence, and considering the single physical life you're blessed to live, and the limited time granted at that, it's a waste to not know or want to appreciate each passing moment you can.

So today, take some time to just stop. Stop anything and everything, any time you can. Stop and simply focus on the moment. Take it all in, see it as clearly as able, and experience it to the fullest. Your journey has taken you across a vast distance, spanning oceans, valleys, maybe deserts and jungles, and even up a mountain... You should have witnessed and experienced some amazing moments in your life thus far... Did you truly appreciate them?

Cherish each and every single moment you're alive to witness and experience life and be thankful to the Lord for them. Use your time on this Earth wisely, for each moment is a unique experience, and all - both good and bad - are precious to us. After all, they make us who we are.

WARRIOR IN A GARDEN

"A student said to his master: 'You teach me fighting, but you talk about peace. How do you reconcile the two?' The master replied: 'It is better to be a warrior in a garden than to be a gardener in a war.'" In other words, it's better to be able to fight and win than to become a victim of circumstance. This is the mentality behind the path warriors throughout history have chosen, and something that should have been instilled within you by now as well.

Understand this... The second you made a commitment to your journey, you began the process of taking the path of the warrior. Warriors are forged in the fires of hardship and adversity, hardened by trial and tempered by experience. Warriors spend a lifetime in the preparation and betterment of the self for the purpose of service to something greater than themselves. They endure these things, not out of lust or joy in them, but out of love for that which they've committed to serve...

Warriors strive to be better each day so that they may serve successfully when needed most.

Sure, one day a warrior may be called upon to serve in conflict, and while laying your life on the line for the protection and defense of what you love is the ultimate form of service, make zero mistake about it... No man wishes for peace MORE than the warrior. True warriors train in the hopes that they may never be forced to serve, yet if they must, that they will be victorious. True warriors, above all else, wish for peace... And the best way to maintain that peace is to be the deadliest warrior in the garden. After all, a true warrior goes forth into battle, not because we hate what stands before us... But because we love that which we protect behind us.

Yet in this regard, the life of a warrior is one of contradiction. You train to fight but wish for peace. This can often lead to internal conflict within the warrior themselves, and where there is conflict, there is perversion of purpose and destruction of progress. We all have a garden within ourselves, and before we can reconcile the conflicts we encounter in life, we must reconcile first the conflict within ourselves. A warrior must quiet the mind, and calm the heart and soul, in order to master their craft, and therein rests both the answer and the challenge of the path of a warrior.

Being a warrior in a garden means calming the self so as not to destroy the peace around you, that your clear mind might allow you the ability to maintain peace within you, and that you refuse to be a victim of circumstance. If your thoughts are corrupted by chaos, it will reflect outwardly, and the turbulence of the mind and heart will become the wrath of the body. Your garden will be destroyed by a storm of your own making, and that's the reality of the struggle true warriors face in their quest to be of service.

Today, consider carefully what it means to be a "Warrior in a Garden", and the realities of what it takes to maintain peace both within and without despite training for war. You have to reconcile the two to maintain sanity, but make no mistake about it, once you've heeded the call, and completed the transformation, you shall never return to what you were once before. Forever a warrior you shall be, so you might as well be the deadliest warrior in the garden.

NO FINGER POINTING

Isaiah (KJV) - 5:8, 5:20-23

"Woe unto those who make the pursuit of money and material things their only drive in life... Woe to those who suggest evil is good, who believe themselves wiser and are therefore unteachable, who live only to party, who make nothing but excuses, and who try to justify their actions..."

Isaiah (KJV) - 6:5

"Then said I, Woe is me! For I am undone; because I am a man of unclean lips, and I dwell in the midst of a people of unclean lips: for mine eyes have seen the King, the Lord of hosts."

In other words, woe is me for pointing fingers and blaming others, for refusing to listen to those wiser than myself and for being hypocritical. For I am just as sinful and without blame, and I should be focusing more on myself and less on others.

In the book of Isaiah, Isaiah spent a lot of time in chapter five pointing fingers at others and condemning their actions, words, and lifestyles... Only to realize in chapter six that he was among them much the same. He understood that it's not his place to judge where he too has fallen short, and he openly admits it, thus allowing him to be cleansed and move forward.

Today, take some serious time to consider this... How often are YOU quick to judge others? How often do you do so without even knowing the whole truth? How often do you refuse to listen and understand other people simply out of bias or arrogance? How often do you condemn people for the same things you are guilty of yourself? The points made in Isaiah chapter five are still correct... That those who think money is all there is to life, those claim sins are "good", those who falsely believe no one can teach them anything, those who refuse responsibility and accountability, and make excuses to justify their sins, are all wrong... But is it our place to point the finger when you KNOW there are areas in YOUR life that need improvement just as much?

Leadership development is the NEVER-ENDING, WILLFUL, Purposeful Development of the SELF, and this means we should be working to better what's inside before taking actions on the outside. Too often we try to "Do before we ARE", and judge others for perceived shortfalls - even without knowing them! Yet I argue, every branch of the military argues, every single leadership course out there argues... And so does God's Word to argue... That we should "Be BEFORE we Do".

To be EFFECTIVE as a leader, you have to BE the example... Instead of casting stones, BE the example you want to see in others. LEAD by example, and the world will follow.

PRACTICE

The mission is at hand, a clear goal is defined, and the clock has started... Are you ready?

Being successful is all about practice. It's all about the hours, days, weeks, and sometimes even years spent building up to the moment where the culmination of your efforts are finally put into action. No one ever achieved anything meaningful by simply dreaming of success. No, they punched the clock, they hit the ground running, they push through the pain, they put in the hours every day, and they prepared to the best of their abilities for the day when they can finally put their skills to the test. So, when you're standing there at the break of dawn, engines fired up, and ready to embark, that moment is NOT the time to start asking yourself if you're capable... If you're ready. No. THAT is the time to KNOW you're ready.

Practice makes achievement possible. Most often reaching the goal will come down to your ability to perform when it matters most. When the odds are pitted against you and times are the toughest. When you're called upon to execute the mission, it will often come in the midst of a sea of chaos and a large amount of uncertainty attached to it. Time and again the seemingly impossible will be asked of you, yet your practice, planning, and preparation can turn the seemingly impossible into the very possible indeed. Your ability to be dependable and reliable, time-on-target +/- 30 seconds, despite the odds, is a direct result of the degree to which you pursued honing your knowledge, abilities, and skills prior to that moment.

No one climbs a mountain without training or preparedness. No one becomes a pilot, a diver, an astronaut, an athlete, a scientist, a doctor or a teacher, a soldier or a sailor, without dedicated practice in time spent training and preparing to qualify and become those things. And even then, not one person truly becomes successful at being those things without continued dedicated practice striving toward never-ending development and mastery thereafter. Since there is no such thing as "perfect" – making the old saying "practice makes perfect" inaccurate – therefore, on-going practice striving for constant improvement is how we raise the bar of standards and achieve great and meaningful things.

Today, ask yourself... The sun has peaked the horizon, the call came in, the engines are hot, and blades are turning... You're geared up and the clock is ticking... The mission has started and it's time to rock and roll... Are. You. Ready? Up until this point, all the time you've put in has filled a logbook of practice. Getting ready, training hard, preparing and planning, so that when the time comes to execute and engage, you're ready, willing, and able to succeed. If the mission were to drop right now, and you had to execute, and you had to question yourself for even a split-second whether or not you're "ready" ... You should know at that point you're not. So, before that time comes, practice diligently so that you KNOW you can succeed. Be confident. Be competent. Be Exceptional. And come back successful.

APPROACH LIGHTS

Sometimes you need a little help to guide you along the way toward your goal. While personal growth and professional development may be self-motivated, individual journeys that only you can take for yourself, this in no way implies that we will always be able to discover the best paths to take or the best answers to solve the challenges we encounter on our own as well. Since self-betterment is a never-ending process, we must acknowledge that even the most experienced individuals are neither experts in all matters or without need of guidance along the way. And to prove this point, we need look no further than the approach lights installed at the ends of airfield runways the world over.

Approach lights at airports are humble reminders that even the most qualified individuals can't reach success without the help of others. Beacons of lights strobing toward the direction of a safe landing, they help us spot airfields from a distance, so we know where to go and where to land. They help us see and identify the runway through the darkness, and they guide us safely to touchdown after we've reached our decision level. After a long flight, halfway around the world, merely spotting approach lights in the distance is an appreciated and welcomed sight, giving us assurance that we're on the right path.

Approach lights in the aviation world act a lot like the mentors we all need throughout our lives. Mentors help keep us on track and provide careful guidance when we either don't know where to go or are unsure of the next path to take. No one has all the answers, and there isn't a person alive capable of achieving without the help of others along the way. We all need careful mentorship and guidance, even leaders, in order to grow and reach new heights. It doesn't matter how high up on your mountain you've managed to climb, how many trials and hardships you've encountered along the way, at some point in everyone's journey, we reach the limits of what we are capable of doing on our own. If we ever want to progress any further, we need a mentor to help guide us, to help us make good decisions, to keep us in check when we're straying from the best path, and to provide both feedback and reality checks when needed most.

Today, take some time to consider – if you haven't already – seeking out a mentor for your own journey. Someone who's been where you are, who's walking the path ahead of you, and who has the well-rounded knowledge, skills, abilities, experience, and character necessary to be a good mentor to you. You can have more than one but consider at least seeking out and finding one.

No one is fully capable of doing everything completely on their own, and at some point, we all reach the end of what we're capable of by ourselves. When we hit that barrier, like approach lights in the distance, a good mentor can become the beacon that shows you the way to a safe landing. After all, even the most qualified individuals are incapable of achieving success without the help of others along the way.

THE FINAL APPROACH

The Final Approach is a short window of time where your intention is to attempt a landing. Landing an aircraft is inherently the most difficult aspect of learning to fly, and this task is considered variable at best. Always a requirement, never an option, on a good day it's merely a matter of developed skill, but on a bad day, it can become a high-risk test of nerves and sound judgment. Yet no matter the time or conditions, it is in this moment where we typically find out who we truly are inside.

Those last few seconds can be the most unnerving and intimidating for many people, and it is in those exact moments in time when your true self comes out into the open. Will you touchdown safely? Will you have a smooth rollout? Will sudden obstacles invade your path? Will you be able to make immediate decisions based on changing environments? How will you handle the exponential buildup of stress as each moment passes and the ground gets closer? The growing number of potential factors increases rapidly as you make your approach to the target, and the knowledge that at any moment something catastrophic could occur has a strong ability to unmask every hidden character, from the wannabe's and cowards to the humble true professionals.

Yet, the final approach of landing an aircraft is merely one example of this particular type of moment that individuals encounter throughout their lifetime. Indeed, there exist many sobering and unnerving moments in life exactly like this example. These "make it or break it" moments can bring out the best or worst in us all, they show us – and others – who we truly are inside, and they're valuable because sometimes even we don't know how we'll act in the face of encountering such situations, especially if we've never encountered a particular situation prior.

Today's a day to reflect on similar moments you may have encountered in your own lifetime. Moments where minutes turned into fractions of a second to possibly react to any number of potential catastrophes that may or may not occur in the next instant. Moments where tensions magnified as windows of opportunities for alternative courses of action narrowed exponentially with every passing second, and where expectations to perform successfully remained despite the challenges present before you. Reflect in all honesty with yourself... How did you act?

While the act of landing an aircraft successfully is a routine action performed to a set standard for aviators, most of the time these kinds of moments are encountered rarely and at random – meaning most people are caught completely unaware and unprepared when they do. However, when we look closely at the individual as they are in the midst of encountering a stressful "final", we find those who have a more mature, calm, collected frame of mind are typically those who have spent significant time in practice, living outside of their comfort zone, becoming fully comfortable with the idea of being uncomfortable.

So, if you find your previous reactions were ones of fear or cowardice, fret not... For now, you've identified an opportunity for growth. Practice makes perfect, and it doesn't matter the level of difficulty you encounter when you're on final intending to land... You're still expected to perform at your finest. It's the developed ability to do so that separates the Exceptional from the Mediocre.

WHAT YOU FILL YOUR LIFE WITH

Second Timothy, 2:4 (KJV) - No man that warreth entangleth himself with the affairs of this life, that he may please him who hath chosen him to be a soldier.

Just as people are the product of their environments, so are our thoughts and desires the product of what we feed the heart and mind. Therefore, ask yourself... Do you struggle with anger? Depression? Malice or hate? Do you swear or curse others? Do you find your life filled with unnecessary struggles, unjust hardships, and hurtful wrongs? Is there violence, corruption, envy, intolerance, closed-minded biases, and more, haunting your thoughts or actions?

If you answered "yes" to any of these, next ask yourself... What are you listening to? Reading? Watching? Or surrounding yourself with?

The music of the world, the popular trends, the social fads, the movies, video games, news media, politics, advertisements, pressures, and even the indoctrinations of our educational institutions, can all be evil, vile, detestable, and destructive to our minds, hearts, and souls. The great majority of the time they are filled with messages that preach violence, hatred, envy, lust, theft and more. They teach and preach that crime is acceptable, that social trends and fads are "ok", that we should idolize false heroes, that drugs and gangs are cool, that life should be "fair", that social justice and equity are somehow logical, and that any who disagree with you should be silenced.

In the course of trying to walk a good and just path in life, without a guidon to follow, we are so easily led astray. And worse, is we allow our children to consume these things and be corrupted themselves too. Thus, we invite and indoctrinate yet another generation to become filled with evil. What's sad is that the freedoms and liberties we enjoy, and the good in the world, is only ever one generation away from extinction.

The true warrior on the good and just path leads by example. Worry not about the flaws and faults of others. Ignore the pop music, get rid of your tv's, dismiss the idols and refuse the biased and agenda-driven news media your attention... Put down the addictive phone filled with apps and games and social media feeds, and focus on YOUR life.

Today, take some very serious time to account for and understand what you choose to surround yourself with. Actually, take the time to focus on what you're listening to, watching, reading, and repeating to others. If you find you're surrounded by a toxic environment of evils, look closely... I guarantee it's destroying you from the inside out, and it's more than likely spreading to your family, friends, and a new generation too. If you find that's the case in your life, perhaps it's time you chose to get away from and get rid of all of those horrible things in your life and make start focusing on a real, positive change instead.

VIRTUES

As leaders on a never-ending journey seeking continuous self-betterment, we strive daily to be the example of what "right" looks like. We strive to be the change we want to see in the world around us, and to provide a guiding light for those who follow us. Yet it's easy to say, and far more difficult to do.

Just as we discussed in previous chapters, you have to "be" before you can "do". The development of your inner self reflects outwardly, and the example that you set for others to see is ultimately a reflection of the kind of person you truly are deep inside. Since our actions determine our character, it is our foundational moral standards we have cemented at our core that ultimately guide the determination of our actions. As such, it's extremely important to understand what virtues we value and what virtues we currently maintain so that we can work to align the two, thus allowing the development of the inner self that guides our outward actions that determine our character.

Those "moral standards" at our core are our "virtues". Virtues are traits or qualities that are deemed ethically and morally good and just, and thus valued as foundational principles of personal characteristics held in high esteem, worth, and desirability, both in one's self and in others. People who express virtuous behaviors maintain high moral standards regardless of the position they are placed within, and regardless of the possible consequences, their choices may have. Courage, Honesty, Mercy, Temperance, Sincerity, Love, Faith, Humility, Prudence, Reliability, Patience, Wisdom, Kindness, and Forgiveness. Virtues like these SHOULD rest at the core of our inner selves, and they are the guides that sway our decisions to take one course of action over another. They are our own inner guiding light that shows us the way forward, even if there's no personal benefit in that path.

Today, take some time to meditate inwardly and discover what virtues you maintain. You'll have to look honestly at your character to discover them... Willingly, and whole-heartedly reflecting at the actions you've taken in the past and the motives behind those actions, in order to discover the influence behind those motives. Do you routinely exhibit one or more of the virtues listed above? Can you identify them and tie them directly to moments where they guided your decisions towards good and just courses of action? Can you clearly define others not listed? Or do you find in your honest reflection that you're lacking virtues to shape your character with?

Our journey toward growth and the achievement of success in life must always remain all-encompassing. While we work to grow stronger, fit, flexible, capable, and more agile, it must be understood that these words do not apply only to the physical. As stated in previous chapters, we must seek to grow the physical, the mental, and the spiritual together, to grow the total-self, if we're ever going to reach our hopes and dreams, and that includes defining and aligning the virtues we require to become the kind of leader capable of achieving great and meaningful things.

OVERCONFIDENCE CAN RUIN IT ALL

It's one thing to be confident in your knowledge, skills, and abilities to achieve the mission, to reach the goal, to be successful, but it's another thing entirely to allow blind arrogance and bias to lead you into a state of overconfidence. Overconfidence places the mission, the team, and yourself at risk through failure to understand and acknowledge potential shortcomings or impending disasters, or a refusal to humbly admit faults in the face of tangible evidence or failures. It leads to a belief that you think you already know everything, making you unteachable, unapproachable by peers and mentors alike, and unreceptive to alternative options or opinions.

Overconfidence is a psychological bias that stems from a false assumption that an individual is superior to others, due to their own false sense of skill, talent, knowledge, experience, or self-belief. The most common manifestations of overconfidence are: over ranking, the illusion of control, timing optimism, and the desirability effect, yet overconfidence has also been attributable to manipulative efforts towards others, while simultaneously dismissing actual facts and data, for the purpose of self-service and personal gain.

Additionally, Self-Serving Biases tend to magnify the development and presence of overconfidence. These types of biases cause people to attribute positive outcomes to perceived "skill" and negative outcomes to an assumption of "luck". In other words, people who express a degree of overconfidence tend to attribute the cause of something to whatever is in our own best interest. Many of us can recall times where we've undertaken a task and decided that if everything went according to plan it was due to skill, but if things went the other way then it must have just been bad luck.

Today is a day to reflect on how much you have grown since your journey began and consider for a second... Have you started developing a degree of overconfidence as a result of your growth? Overconfidence can be a dangerous attitude to have as it can result in disastrous and/or destructive consequences both for yourself and for the team. It can lead you into making decisions founded on ignorance, and it can take you down a dangerous path no reasoned person would tread. It can destroy your reputation as a leader once people decide you've become arrogant and unapproachable. If you're unwilling to listen to understand people with different positions and opinions than yourself do to a false sense of superiority, you'll quickly find yourself surrounded by conflict of your own creation, and alone with no one in your corner but yourself.

If you ever come to a difficult task and think you can accomplish it just fine, while your peers are second-guessing their own success, perhaps you need to check yourself. If you ever find yourself arguing a point based on an emotional position instead of a factual, evidence-based one, you're probably infected with overconfidence. Remember... It's one thing to be confident in your competencies and capabilities to be successful, and this is highly encouraged... But it's another thing entirely to blindly believe you can do anything, know everything, and no one can teach you or tell you differently.

BE A TEAM, NOT A HERD

When people copy and follow what other people are doing, and then falsely perceive that they are making independent choices and decisions, when in reality, they are not, this is called the "Herd-Mentality Bias". Further, although capable of existing independently, herd-mentalities have the ability to produce "Group-Think" (also known as "The Bandwagon Effect") as a strong by-product, which is the tendency to do (or believe) things simply because many other people do (or believe) the same. Both of these are dangerous and disruptive to the potential success of teams, and they are strong indicators of a lack of intellectual capacity amongst team members.

People who are easily influenced by emotion, rather than by independent critical analysis, are highly susceptible to indoctrination into a herd mentality and groupthink, and you often find these types of individuals unaware that they have fallen into these traps. Case-in-point... Our society today is vastly polarized by tribal-like fringe mindsets on two far-removed sides, where most people seem to refuse to believe they have reduced themselves to the level of sheep due to allowing hardened emotionally driven biases drive their thinking and actions for them. Yet I submit to you that no reasonably intelligent person would knowingly readily agree with a group simply because the group says and does things that align with their own personal biases. Likewise, no reasonably intelligent person would knowingly allow themselves to be brainwashed and indoctrinated into a mindless herd, that preaches mindless rhetoric, and that promotes mindless actions.

No... Intelligent people challenge ideas, perspectives, thoughts, and actions, especially if agreeable, to remove bias and check for validity. Intelligent people routinely check themselves to see if they are truly thinking and acting independently.

The simple fact of the matter is, you should focus on building and being a "team", and REFUSE to become a member of a "herd". Teams aren't herds; they're not sheep. They are a group of individuals, fully capable of thinking and acting independently for themselves, but who willingly work collectively toward a common goal. And since high-performance teams are made up of reasonably intelligent individuals who should be checking their biases and engaging in actions and decision-making through critical analysis instead of through emotion-driven biases, high-performance teams, therefore, should regularly check themselves for the development of collectivistic herd-mentalities and groupthink just the same.

Today, take some time to check YOURSELF for indoctrination into a tribal-like polarized fringe-mentality herd. Reflect on your recent past interactions with others – both within and outside of your team(s) – and be honest about your actions, motives, thoughts, interactions, and words. Check yourself for strong biases and be honest if you've allowed your emotionally driven biases to unintelligently drive your thoughts and actions for you, instead of engaging in a well-reasoned, intellectual way.

Understand this... Your job as both a leader and a member of the team is to promote and capitalize on the individual capabilities each member brings to the table for the benefit of the team's success, and that includes your own place within the team as well. You can't do that if you're all mindless sheep in a herd. Each person brings something unique capability to the team – be it a thought or idea, an insight or understanding, special skills or unique experience, and more. If you ever find yourself or your team infected by a herd-mentality and engaging in groupthink, stop and step back... Challenge your perspective immediately, promote independent thought, and allow the best ideas – even middle grounds – to rise to the top.

ADMIT FAULTS AND MOVE ON

There are a great many people who, no matter the circumstances, will absolutely refuse to accept any responsibility for themselves or be held personally accountable for their actions when facing a negative outcome. Instead, rather than admitting any guilt at all, they will use any number of logical fallacies to appeal to others in order to remove a sense of fault or blame from themselves and displace it unto someone or something else.

Called the "Saving-Face Mentality", people who exhibit this mentality will often turn to impression-management techniques in times of failure to attempt to still come across to others in a good light despite any possible faults. As such, nothing will ever be "their fault". Any time anything goes wrong, doesn't go their way or according to the plan, it will always be someone or something else's fault. Never them; they are, for some reason, never directly to blame for any shortcoming that any evidence may show they are directly responsible for.

Plain and simple and right to the point here, people who refuse to be held accountable for their actions, and who refuse to accept any responsibility for their faults by shifting blame or outright pointing the finger at anyone and everyone or everything BUT themselves, are untrustworthy and should not be allowed to be members of your team. If they aren't capable of owning up to mistakes or shortcomings, and they aren't capable of being team players. This means they will at all times seek to avoid accepting any personal accountability or responsibility for their own actions and decisions when failure or wrongdoings are discovered, and since they only ever think of themselves, they aren't capable of leadership either.

EVERYONE makes mistakes. NO ONE is perfect. We can't lead if we're untrustworthy, and the team will never succeed if its members are incapable of accepting personal responsibility or of holding themselves and each other accountable. No one likes admitting a negative outcome was their fault or that they messed up, but part of being an adult, a team player, and a leader, is being able to willingly admit when you have fallen short. Part of your journey to success is accepting your faults and being willing to admit when you were wrong, so that you can learn from those things and grow, and then MOVE ON. If you aren't capable of at LEAST that much by NOW, then you might as well just start this book over from the very beginning and try again...

There's really no reason to take a whole day to contemplate this concept, it's pretty clear. Grow up. Accept blame when something is your fault. Willingly accept personal responsibility and accountability for your life, your faults, your actions, your words, your behavior, your shortcomings, and more. STOP trying to "save face". Admit where you've made mistakes, learn and grow from them, laugh about them if able, set the example for others to follow, and then move on with the mission. THAT's one of many solid ways to build trust, build character, and BE the example.

LOOK FOR THE WHOLE PICTURE, NOT JUST THE SIDE YOU AGREE WITH

Too often today do we find a great number of people throughout our society emotionally discarding any position or argument they simply disagree with. Across social media, the "unfriend", "unfollow", and "block" actions are taken by the millions on a routine basis. Worse, people will actually "report" the posts of others in a malicious effort to censor the post or the individual (or both) simply because they have childish emotional reactions of disagreement to the content. We find people have a great tendency to willfully refuse to engage with any media (books, news, images, articles, reports, statistics, etc.) that don't readily agree with their own personal biases and beliefs, and this has created a culture of ignorance, unwilling and largely unable to think critically and engage intellectually with concepts of a difficult nature.

Echo-Chambers are rampant today. These are manufactured environments in which a person encounters only beliefs or opinions that coincide with their own so that their existing views are reinforced, and alternative ideas are not considered. The creation of echo-chambers is caused by people habitually choosing to ignore information and facts they simply don't agree with, that don't agree with their personal beliefs, world-view, or position on a given topic, as they purposely seek out only information that confirms or agrees with these things.

Anchoring Biases have become the fallacies of biased arguments as people use pre-existing data as a reference point for all subsequent data, which can skew our decision-making processes. It's a tendency to rely too heavily upon, or "anchor", on one trait or piece of information when making decisions (usually the first piece of information acquired on that subject) while ignoring the whole picture or all the other evidence which contradicts that singular piece of information.

Confirmation Bias, a byproduct of willful ignorance and echo-chamber development, has become a barrier preventing individuals from seeking out real facts and real information, as the tendency to search for, interpret, focus on, and remember only information that confirms one's preconceptions about reality and events.

And worse yet, are the industries that contribute greatly to feeding all these things through the use of Framing Bias. Social media and the news media manipulate information feeds to present only things that agree with the perception they want to promote, the image they want you to see, and the agenda they want to push. They manufacture a fake reality to create a perception about facts and events, present this new "framed" perspective to the public, in order to drive individual and collective decision-making regarding the manufactured perspective presented, rather than tell the whole truth, the whole story, and give all sides, based solely on all the facts, and nothing but the facts. In other words, if someone sees the same facts but presented in different ways, they are likely to come to a different conclusion about an event.

Here's the bottom line...

DO NOT ALLOW YOURSELF TO BECOME A PART OF THIS MALICIOUS TRAP! Do NOT lower and degrade yourself to the level of ignorance and stupidity involved in developing an echo-chamber for yourself. LEARN how to think and reason critically, NOT "emotionally", and seek out the WHOLE picture, not just the side you agree with. ENGAGE with different opinions and perspectives that you inherently disagree with in a well-reasoned and intellectual way! LISTEN to UNDERSTAND, and do NOT simply "hear to respond". Let FACTS and real – unskewed – data CHANGE your opinions and perceptions, and do NOT ignore these things just because you don't agree with them. Don't fall for framed stories and feeds with clearly fallaciously worded headlines designed to grab your attention through the use of emotionally driven biases!

You are BETTER than these things! And your challenge for today is removing these things from your life, as much as possible.

FOCUS ON POSITIVE STRENGTHS, NOT PERCEIVED NEGATIVES

Have you ever heard of the Frequency Illusion, also known as the Baader-Meinhof Phenomenon? In the 1950s, the world was at a height in the Cold War, and the United States government was "seeing Red" everywhere it looked. Russian spies were supposedly everywhere, and people who were previously hailed as patriots routinely found themselves defending their loyalty at accusations of being Communist. The Frequency Illusion happens whenever a word, a name, a color, a number, types of events, or any other thing that has recently come to a person's attention and awareness suddenly seems to appear with improbable frequency shortly afterward. Suddenly the individual discovers this thing or event appearing or happening so much that they believe it's appearing or happening far more than normal. And worse, is that this illusion is especially strong when the thing or event is perceived as something "negative".

When it comes to the human brain, we have a strong tendency to remember, retain, pay attention to, and focus on negative events and behaviors. This has a bit to do with our innate survival instincts, but the result is, that information of a negative nature leaves more of a marked impression in our minds than positive ones do. As a leader, this is important because the frequency illusion, and our strong natural tendency to give more attention to negativity, work hand-in-hand to generate a toxic perception of hostility from within our own team members, when the reality is, there isn't any...

"Hostile Attribution Bias" is the tendency to interpret others' behaviors as having hostile intent, even when the behavior is ambiguous or benign. We see this all the time across social media, don't we? One person makes a statement, and though the statement may have been made without the slightest bit of emotion behind it by the person who wrote it, the person on the other end impresses their own emotional attributions upon the statement and perceives it negatively. This is because the written word has no emotional context of its own unless the writer specifically goes out of their way to include markers, word choices, or symbolism to create it. Well leaders are not immune to this encountering hostile attribution bias when it comes from within their teams either, and they can falsely perceive a subordinate as "hostile" in communication, even when the subordinate has no hostile intent whatsoever, and worse, that the individual has repeated "bad behavior" when they haven't.

Today, take some time to identify "perceived" negativities you think you might be encountering from a teammate, coworker, subordinate, or friend. If you find negative events, attitudes, or behaviors exist, next consider carefully whether you think they have been occurring – even if subtlety – with frequency. If this is the case, now might be a good time to consider if maybe you might be affected by a hostile attribution bias. Everything up to this point in your journey has kept you focused on "hunting the good stuff", on staying positive, and building strength through adversity... Well, now is no different.

Your team can quickly destroy itself from within if biases give members a falsely perceived sense of hostility derived from the illusion of frequent negativity. The best way to combat this is to focus on the strengths your team has – both as a team and individually – instead of allowing your attention to be consumed by perceived shortcomings. So, check yourself before you make up your mind that someone is a problem. You might find your perception of that individual has been fooled by false attribution of constant negativities that, in reality, may not actually exist.

TRUTHS ARE NOT EQUAL TO FACTS

A "truth" can be found in individual beliefs and is very often emotionally driven. We seek to determine whether or not something is true based on logical reasoning, and depending on where your starting point is, and using only the knowledge available at the time, what can be determined to be "true" or not can change depending on a large number of variables. What is considered "true" for one person, may not be the same for another, but so long as the reasoning behind it doesn't conclude in a logical fallacy, it's possible to have multiple "truths" from different perspectives about the same subject.

However, facts are things that do not change regardless of individual perception, amount of knowledge, reasoning, personal beliefs or biases, or the passage of time. Facts are based on empirical evidence and are replicable. They can be observed – either directly or indirectly – measured, documented, accounted for, and supported. This is why science focuses on facts and not truths. If you want to focus on and argue over truths, major in philosophy. But if you desire to intelligently understand the universe you exist in, and the world around you, then you must cast aside "truths" in favor of "facts", and allow those facts to alter your opinions, perspectives, biases, and positions.

Individuals who focus primarily on truths are often ruled by their emotions, meaning they allow their emotions to dictate their thoughts and actions for them. They base their perception of reality on how they feel, and often tend seek out only information that supports their feelings while ignoring other information that doesn't, so that they can twist and frame reality to conform to their own personal beliefs. Now, of course, any argument over a subject based on a "truth" must reach a non-fallacious and truthful conclusion, but regardless of whether or not an argument is true, it is still based on an individual's personally biased perspective. And since it's entirely possible to have multiple "truths" from different perspectives, each of which that may or may not agree with each other, all positions over the same subject could be equally correct and equally wrong. Only a position based on facts would be purely correct, and with that, there's the cold, hard reality of the matter... Facts are more important than feelings, and when it comes to your personal growth and leadership development, facts matter.

Individuals who focus on facts allow evidence (not feelings) to alter their perception of reality. They will hold off on forming an opinion or taking a position until they educate themselves on the facts. If they held a previous preference or bias, intelligent individuals will allow facts to change those preferences or biases to align with reality, not the other way around. In doing so, they are able to form an educated understanding about a subject based on critical analysis and make good decisions as a result.

Today, take some time to question what "truths" you hold and assert in your daily life, and then question if those "truths" are grounded in "facts". You may discover you assert logical truths quite frequently, but that little to none of them are factually based, but instead, emotionally based positions. The simple fact of the matter is, "truths" are not equal to "facts", but "facts" can be used to derive "truths". Therefore, as part of your never-ending journey to climb your mountain, understanding the difference between the two is critical to your ability to grow. Seek out facts and let them become the basis for your positions. After all, facts are more important than feelings.

PEOPLE ARE A LIBRARY

Getting to know someone is like reading every book in a library. We all have history behind us – years of history – and while they say you shouldn't judge a book by its cover, why do we tend to judge people we don't even know before we get to know them first?

You know... People are more than just one book. They're a library, a multifaceted collection of knowledge, experiences, abilities, and skills that make up the story of their lives... And it most certainly takes each of us a long period of time to truly get to know each other. Our lifetime of history brings to the table a combination of both common and unique abilities and traits that are still being written and developed with each passing day, and despite the volumes contained therein, we have a strong tendency to pass judgment on a person based on a tiny sliver of who they are as a whole.

If the story of a person's life as a whole could fill a library, we have a strong tendency to judge most people based off of only one or two books, most often ones we don't even like or agree with at that. Yet I argue, just because we might find we don't like or agree with one or two of the books in their entire collection, doesn't mean we'll hate or disagree with them all. This is why it's so important not to base our judgments on one or two aspects we think we don't like about someone else.

Face it... People are more than just one story, we all have a lifetime of history behind us, and even those books you think you don't agree with, they are important too... For they make up the whole of that person and can teach you something if you'd simply listen. After all, the mark of true intelligence and maturity is the ability to engage criticality with ideas you don't agree with, and accept truth, facts, and a better path when presented with them.

So, today's a day to think about all the people you decided you didn't like throughout your life based on a disagreement you had over something about them you thought you didn't like or agree with. We have ALL done this, and to deny it would be a complete lie. So just admit you've done it, then consider this... If you would have stopped judging and started listening, and if you would have stopped dismissing and started finding commonalities, might things have turned out differently? And if they could have, might even your life today have turned out a little bit differently? Perhaps better or more enriched by getting to know that person better?

Remember that, the next time you think of judging someone before you get know them, you could be destroying a future opportunity, a future friendship, a solid source of council, a good source of knowledge and skills, or even the keys you need to be successful. Everyone has something in their lives – opinions, positions, quirks, personality traits, etc. – we might not like or disagree with... But they all have something they can teach us, and if you dig deeper than those one or two books, you might find a library of commonalities, agreements, and valuc on the other side.

DON'T LEAD BY "FEELINGS"

You would think that, given enough time and resources, most people would make good decisions and judge things logically. However, research proves that even when given all the time in the world, most people still let their personal biases and feelings lead their decision-making and make their judgments for them. This is because the human brain has a strong tendency to revert to using subconscious cognitive shortcuts known as "heuristics" when we're faced with making either a decision or forming a judgment, and this is one reason why many intelligent people still end up making bad decisions or judge things incorrectly.

While heuristics can be good when it comes to applying lessons learned, the vast majority of the time, heuristics are based on personal feelings, inaccurate information, and personal biases. This means that, even when faced with important decisions, and even when given all the opportunity in the world to form a qualified and intelligent judgment, people still tend to let their emotions guide them instead of facts and data. Of course, this is very bad when it comes to trying to help mentor and educate people, when making leadership decisions in the field, or even when trying to engage in tough conversations about important topics.

Essentially, our personal feelings create a barrier that prevents critical thinking and constructive engagement from taking place. They can effectively close off an individual from learning something new from someone or something else they emotionally disagree with, they can prevent people from growing as a leader and executing effective leadership, and they have a strong tendency to stifle constructive intellectual discourse and engage with new ideas and differences of opinion by anchoring individuals in previously held biases.

We most often don't always have all the time in the world to make a "good" decision, but it's not a good practice to make snap judgments about people and situations that are inaccurate or completely false either. Instead, when it comes to leadership and our own personal self-betterment, the simple truth about how to make good decisions and good judgments is to refuse to allow your "feelings" to be your guide. Set your biases aside and learn to engage critically with the world around you and the information you're presented without allowing your emotions to get in the way.

Today, think carefully about some of the important decisions and snap judgments you've made in the past. We've all allowed our emotion-driven biases to guide our decision-making and judgments about both people and situations in the past, but the results end up poor, inaccurate, incorrect, and flawed most of the time. When it comes to making logical, well-reasoned decisions, your "feelings" are often the enemy that will lead you astray, prevent you from progress, and create division and friction as a result. As a leader, this can end up leading the team to failure, or worse, and as a person on the journey striving toward achievement and success, allowing your emotions to sway your judgments can and will set you back.

What's the lesson here? We shouldn't allow our "feelings" to become our leadership style, nor allow them to guide our decisions or judgments either. If you want to grow and lead effectively, learn to set your feelings aside and engage critically with the world around you.

EMBRACE FAILURE

Some people see failure as the worst thing in the world, and some people preach failure as "never an option". Yet no matter how you feel about the idea of failure, the truth is that everyone fails at some point in their lives. We've all encountered instances where we didn't pass a test, make the team, get accepted, or receive a reward or recognition for our efforts. We all know what it's like to put forth your best only to fail in the end. But guess what... For all you out there who hate the idea of failing, you're missing out on something highly important that comes from failure... The opportunity for success.

That's right. Success often comes from the ashes of failing, because failure can teach us vital lessons we didn't get before. These are ideas and concepts we didn't think of, alternative paths we didn't see, or even processes we didn't realize existed or were possible, all of which we can use to perform better next time. From failure, we have an opportunity to learn, to grow, and outperform, and in that respect, failure is really nothing more than a steppingstone to help us achieve. In fact, the only truly bad form of failure is failing to try again or try at all.

If you spent all your efforts trying to avoid failure, you'll most likely fail due to missing key aspects or never learning key lessons that could show you a better path. Failure avoidance often leads to plateaus in growth and mediocre results due to limiting efforts below peak capabilities. Fear of failure inhibits your ability to go all-out when it matters most or in the endeavor of striving for meaningful achievements, and the results are often below expectations and unsatisfying to the individual and the team.

Sure, it sucks to fail, especially when you put forth a great deal of effort into striving to succeed. Further, we can clearly identify some types of failures that we should try to mitigate and seek to prevent, types that result in injuries, loss of equipment, or loss of life... Yet good leaders know the hidden value of failure, and individuals of great character and high-performance teams alike embrace failure in the pursuit of accomplishing great and meaningful things. They use failure as a measure to gauge progress, to evaluate their efforts and find ways to improve, and ultimately as a tool to guide them along the path to success.

Today, take some time to reflect on your journey as a whole so far... You left a beach in a far-off land, crossed an ocean of adversity, walked through deserts, forests, and a deep valley, and climbed a mountain with no summit, striving for greater and greater heights, all to improve yourself, develop yourself, and reach your hopes and dreams... You've likely encountered many failures along the way, but looking back at the world far below, you should realize you didn't let those setbacks stop you. Just look at how far you've gone! Just look at those who've seen your example and followed suit! What lessons from your failures have you learned? Have others learned?

Today... Be thankful for your failures, and embrace them, for those experiences have made you better now than you ever were before. If you've learned anything from past failures it should be that you can handle failure and rise from it to be successful... And that is a lesson that will help you reach the stars.

STRESS CAN HELP YOU SUCCEED

As discussed back on Day 68, stress can be either physical or mental and can be either good or bad. While that Day focused on learning to identify, let go of, and decompress from negative mental stressors in your life, not all stress is "bad". In fact, good stress is not only healthy, it keeps you at the tip of the spear. It helps push you to continuously be better, to constantly seek growth and improvement, and to stay in top performance capabilities. These are things such as daily physical training and exercise, challenging assignments and projects, and continuous reading and learning. Yet, in order for these types of stressors to stay good and healthy, they need to be encountered regularly and managed properly.

Proper stress management can help you succeed by increasing your performance levels beyond your comfort zone, while still yet maintaining them within your range of capabilities, thus allowing you to excel and grow. According to the Yerkes-Dodson Law, there is an empirical relationship between physiological and psychological arousal and performance. The more we enjoy the task we're undertaking or state we're encountering, the better we perform. Yet this is only up to a certain point... The Yerkes-Dodson Law is a bell-curve after all and diminishing returns on performance occurs whenever our interest and/or enjoyment exceeds our capacity to maintain positive performance. This gives us a range to work within, whereby our performance zone rests above our comfort zone but below the apex of the curve, and just beyond our peak performance capability is where the curve falls.

This brings us to the next point... Encountering good stress with frequency and regularity.

Our "comfort zone" rests at the bottom of our performance range. This is because we're not inducing any stressors while operating within our comfort zone. Remember back on Day 47 when we talked about your Bubble of Comfort – your Comfort Zone – and how it holds you back from success? This is because without good stress pushing you to perform at higher levels – levels you're fully capable of but that exist beyond your comfort zone – you're not growing. Good stress exists beyond our place of comfortability, and success is only possible when we strive to reach it. As such, we're only capable of success by leaving our comfort zone, and therefore, we should be seeking to live permanently outside of our comfort zone. We should be striving to set up shop and live in a constant state of discomfort, and vacation in our comfort zone only when needed, so that we can allow good and positive stressors to constantly grow us.

Today, take some time to contemplate the good stress you SHOULD have in your daily life. Think about things you choose to engage with, like daily exercise, challenging mental puzzles or problems, projects and hobbies, challenging work assignments, reading a new book, and more. Consider if maybe you aren't "challenged" enough, and if not, your growth has likely stagnated. Remember that as we grow, our comfort zone grows to, and what was once considered a challenge no longer is. What was once a good stressor has become routine. Our goal should be an ongoing striving to become a little bit better than the "you" of the day before. So, ask yourself... Are you living and thriving outside of your comfort zone? Do you have enough good stress to push you to excel? If not... Perhaps it's time to find some and start.

ENTITLEMENT WILL KILL
YOUR PROGRESS

There's a toxic mentality that is capable of springing up in anyone, and it can even develop in and corrupt people who have worked hard to achieve a measure of success throughout their lives. People who have put in 20 or 30 years in a career, worked hard for something and have seen measurable results, and those who have reached higher levels on the ladder, are highly susceptible to believing "they've done their time", "they've done their part", and NOW the world "owes" them something... Known commonly today as the "Entitlement Mentality", a sense of "entitlement" is a toxic disease that only serves as a wall to block your path. It will kill your journey because the truth is, life owes you nothing.

A mentality of entitlement stems from a refusal to accept responsibility for yourself. If you refuse to believe you are responsible for yourself, then that means you believe everyone else must, therefore, be held responsible for you. You believe your neighbor must be held responsible to take care of you, and when you find they refuse, you believe it's acceptable to use government to attempt to forcefully make them take care of you. Such a position is founded in the idea you believe you're entitled to life, basic needs, wealth, care, and enjoyment, and since you refuse to hold yourself responsible for earning and/or maintaining those things, you unjustly place the burden of their provision on the world, and scream at the world to provide them to you. And when you find the world against your tyrannous ideas of forced confiscation and redistribution, and when you don't get what you falsely believe you're "entitled" to, you claim victimhood.

This is a common theme that has been mentioned several times so far, but it cannot be expressed enough. You're not "entitled" to anything. Not success, nor money, nor healthcare or basic needs, not food or water, not happiness or even life itself. Every single thing you gain in life must be earned, and every single thing you earn should be cherished as a blessing. Understanding that life owes you nothing, means you inherently understand you – and you alone – are responsible for yourself and your own happiness. Acceptance of personal responsibility leads to taking actions to earn the things you desire in life, and this translates to a willingness to work hard to ultimately achieve success at reaching your goals, hopes, and dreams.

Today is a day to count your blessings and reaffirm acceptance of personal responsibility and accountability. You may have achieved some measure of success so far in your life, but the world is not responsible for your success, nor is it responsible for maintaining it for you either. Even after you've earned a little of it, you must still earn the right to keep it. You're not entitled any amount of respect just for achieving something, nor for the hard work you've put in, nor for the position or status you may have attained. Even after you've achieved something great, if you refuse to take responsibility for maintaining it, you can still lose it in the very next moment. No one is immune from developing an Entitlement Mentality, so remind yourself that you're not, count your blessings, refuse victimhood, and take personal responsibility.

HIT THE GROUND RUNNING
EVERY DAY

Our willingness to take on the challenge of our journey is fed by our internalized motivational desire to succeed, and little by little, we begin to build momentum as we make progress toward our goals. Yet, motivation tends to start off high in most cases, but then gradually decline over time. After all, it's easy to lose momentum when the ground starts getting steep. As we make progress, what was once new and exciting, slowly turns into the normal and routine. Before long, our motivation can dwindle as the days become mundane, and if we're not careful, we can quickly find ourselves losing interest in the pursuit of reaching our hopes and dreams.

Keeping our motivation high is a requirement if we're ever to achieve something meaningful and worthwhile. Therefore, recharging our motivation should become a daily morning routine. We won't always wake up filled with ambition and itching to get going, but just like the other routines you've developed to keep your mind, body, and spirit fed daily (reading, exercise, study, reflection, prayer, etc.), "getting" motivated is no less important. That's why, no matter how you're "feeling" on that day, hit the ground running regardless.

There will be days when hopping out of bed and getting straight to work will be easy. When you're highly motivated and can't wait to get started. But after a while, it'll be tricky to keep that momentum going. When that happens, you'll have to force yourself to be motivated to press on, and there's a variety of techniques you can use to help you get going... You could try changing your perspective about the tasks/mission for the day.

You can try altering the order of the tasks you need to perform if able. Or you could try writing down your major goals, then break them down into smaller goals, and check them off as completed so you can visually see your progress. You could also try switching up what you choose to work on with regularity. Change the routine, break off main goals, and work on side quests for a bit, then return to the main goals once again, recharged and refreshed.

Whatever approach you take, you should be able to tackle something in the short-run, and it should always end up leading you back on track toward your ultimate goal(s). In this manner, a clear path to achievement for the day should become visible, thus offering you daily purpose and direction to work with, and no matter how you're feeling at the time, a reachable goal should give you the motivation you need to sprint forward to success.

Today, consider the importance of looking for and finding reasons to hit the ground running every day, even on those days when you're not particularly feeling up to it. It's short-sighted to believe a lifelong journey toward self-betterment and success will be filled with motivation every single day, and our progress can come to a grinding halt before we even realize it, if we don't find reasons to feed our internal motivation to keep going. When this happens, consider alternative approaches to be productive, and come back to the primary mission afterward. It's easy to say you'll be able to commit to a long journey, but unless you feed your motivation daily, you'll soon find none left to keep you going.

SEEK MENTORSHIP

Imagine taking on a challenge, but despite your best efforts, you can't seem to make serious progress. You keep chipping away at it little by little, yet you keep reaching points where you feel lost and unable to move forward, leaving you feeling like you won't be able to overcome it. Yet just when you're considering giving up, you instead turn to someone who once took on a similar challenge and overcame it. They look over your progress so far, offer you a bit of insight into how you can better approach the issue, and to your amazement, you're now able to see things from a different perspective and overcome the challenge for yourself!

Such is the power of good mentorship.

Your life is exactly the same as that challenge, and when it comes to your journey of never-ending self-betterment, you'll very often encounter times when you won't be able to find the answer or discover the best possible path to take in order to overcome the challenges you encounter on your own. This is because we are so familiar with ourselves that we very often can't see where we need improvement or how to judge our own progress. It is in these times that a well-reasoned voice of careful guidance can help us reach new heights, and therefore, at some point in our journey, we need to seek out a mentor we trust and who has more experience than us, to guide us along the right path.

Mentors can keep us on track by helping us progress toward our goals, but they can also be a solid source of encouragement, keeping us motivated along the way too. Acting like a convex mirror posted on a curve in the road of life, mentors are able to show us both the way we came and give us a glimpse of what lies ahead. They can help us determine if we're still on the right path, and if not, what corrections to make, ultimately aiding us in figuring out how to proceed next.

However, it is highly important to keep in mind that mentors can also show us a reflection of ourselves we either aren't able to see or refuse to see otherwise. This is where selecting the right mentor becomes critical. Bad mentorship can tear you down and lead you down a self-destructive path, but good mentorship – despite showing you your own flaws and faults – is able to build you up and guide you toward being better. Good mentors are able to provide us with feedback on our progress and grant us insights we couldn't think of otherwise, vastly improving our capability for growth and keeping us motivated toward success.

Today, consider carefully your own need for positive, well-reasoned mentorship in your life. Mentors are the guideposts that provide us a perspective we are incapable of seeing on our own. Because they are further along in their own journeys, they have experience you don't yet possess and are able to impart wisdom to help you take the next step. Mentors help us grow and improve our potential, allow us to track our progress, stay on the best possible path, and reach our goals. We still have to do the work, but when we become unable to see the way, they can help us discover it, making good mentorship an essential key to our development.

You'll Always Have Room for Improvement

At long last, you've reached the conclusion of this short period of personal reflection and growth. Ninety days may have seemed like a lot at first, but for a certainty, the time has surely flown by. The hope is that you've taken this journey with serious sincerity, enjoyed the challenges encountered along the way, considered carefully each idea and applied them actively to your life, and have grown significantly as a result. Hopefully, you've discovered new things about yourself you didn't know before you began. Hopefully, you've learned you're more capable than previously imagined. And hopefully, you've gained something valuable, which was worth your time and effort in reading this book and applying its daily concepts to your own life.

Yet even if you committed to sincere personal reflection, development, and growth during these past ninety days, the lessons contained herein wouldn't be justified if emphasis wasn't reinforced to their incompletion. Truly it cannot be expressed enough, that your journey has no end. In fact, it's just getting started. Each day only scratched the surface of each thought presented for your consideration, and the exploration of their depths has been left for you to personally discover. There exists a lifetime left remaining for you to build upon, and an unfathomable number of new concepts to reflect upon and lessons to learn, consider, and apply. This book was merely a tool for you to use to get started, and the hope is that you'll continue traveling further, diving deeper, and climbing higher from here on out.

The core lessons of responsibility, accountability, resiliency, strength, fortitude, ingenuity, perseverance, positivity, and more are foundational keys to your ability to be successful in life. These are lessons that warriors throughout history had to learn early in order to survive, protect, and serve, and they apply equally to all people from all walks of life, and all backgrounds, who seek to achieve great and meaningful things in life. You need to KNOW beyond doubt that you can accomplish anything, that no challenge is too great for you to rise up and overcome. There exists no sea too wide, no storm too rough, no valley too deep, and no mountain too high, that you can't cross, weather, tread, or climb, to reach your goals. Time and again we will be confronted with the seemingly impossible along the way, but with some careful planning and preparation, tenacity and a bit of grit, positivity and internalized motivation, you can and WILL succeed.

As time goes on, you're likely to come face-to-face with all new challenges you've never encountered before, and as such, new opportunities for growth beyond what you've become today. These events should be welcomed with open arms, and the difficulty of them embraced like an old friend. For they will make you stronger, wiser, and more capable than you've ever been before. They will mold you into a figure of great character and capable of leadership influence beyond measure. Such is the goal of the journey itself! Never ending, always progressing, you'll ALWAYS have room for further improvement and refinement. Hopefully, you too can appreciate and embrace such an idea... And with that, go forth and do great things.

INDEX

90-Day Readings

Foundation Building Days

Core Development Days

<u>Crossing the Sea of Adversity</u>

Climbing the Mountain with No Summit

ABOUT THE AUTHOR

AJ is a Christian, a retired United States Army NonCommissioned Officer who served in both the U.S. Navy and U.S. Army, and he is a world-traveled American combat veteran. His professional military experience spans the full-spectrum of aviation operations, to include general, tactical, combat, SAR/CSAR/PR and MEDEVAC, VIP/DV operations, teaching, training and instruction, and special operations and special missions aviation operations.

AJ is a fully qualified aircraft mechanic and technician, flight engineer and pilot. He is a certified master SCUBA diver and advanced search & rescue technician, an industry certified compliance officer and technical inspector, and a qualified standardization instructor, evaluator, and trainer. During his professional career, AJ has been blessed with opportunities to work at the local, joint, and multinational levels of operations, working closely with U.S. and allied forces in conducting operations, training, development, and relations-building.

AJ is an author, published researcher, guest lecturer, and public speaker. He is a social and political advocate for the veteran's community as a whole, and enjoys opportunities to teach, coach, mentor, and guide others towards self-betterment and success. He is a graduate of Pennsylvania State University, and is published academically in the fields of sociology and leadership.

On his off time, AJ loves shooting, long-distance rucking, flying, scuba diving, rock wall climbing, motorcycle riding, running, weight and resistance training, swimming, snowboarding, practicing Aikido, photography, adventure seeking, and traveling around the world to meet new people and experience new things. AJ believes "investing in experiences" and "investing in relationships" are keys to investing in your future.

He is always seeking out new knowledge and new opportunities, and believes education and self-betterment are life-long endeavors.

NOTES

NOTES

NOTES

NOTES